THE
FOURTEENTH
YEAR

THE FOURTEENTH YEAR

BY KELLY WATT

Mill City Press, Inc

Some of the names in this book have been
changed to protect the innocent.

The love of a good man can change a person. It can make someone see themself through anothers eyes. Thank you to my wonderful husband, Bruce, for always seeing the best in me. To my children, those I bore and those I didn't. You are amazing human beings.

A special thanks goes out to Connie Johnson and Jennifer Fugal for their beautiful insight into my mind and for helping me put it into words. Thanks to Carla Popko for her excellent organization skills and attention to detail. The three of you are a great source of support and an example of pure love and unselfishness.

CHAPTER 1

*"But whoso shall offend one of these little ones
which believe in me, it were better for him that a
millstone were hanged about his neck, and that he
were drowned in the depth of the sea."*
Matthew 18:6

I feel like I've lived ten lives. Some of them I remember more clearly. Some call for remembering, yet others rumble under my skin. I can forget anything if I really want to. I repeat in my mind, *forget, forget, forget.* I can close a curtain in my brain to keep what is in the front from seeing what is in the back. I have to. My mind doesn't have enough room for everything that's going on, and so I either empty it or store it. I hide parts of my life behind that curtain. It takes some control, but I'm really good at it. I've had to forget a lot.

I've come upstairs to the bathroom of our old house. I stand on the claw-foot tub to push my backpack out the small window. I see the top of our garage and beyond it, the trail I'm going to take through the dusk.

Should I jump out the window or try to escape through the front door? I could probably make it through the opening of the window, but odds are I'd break my legs. I haven't mustered up the courage to leave and risk this getaway being destroyed by an amateur escape plan. Besides, I need my legs more than ever now. I will race like I am running for my life—because I am.

I will have to outmaneuver Carrie through the house. She's no dummy, and I swear I must have my whole plan tattooed on my forehead. She's following me around asking dumb questions like, "Where are you going?"

Like I would ever give up my destination to the enemy. I try to calm her little twelve-year-old mind by sitting down on the couch. It doesn't work. When I turn my head, I catch a glimpse of the sneaky expression on her sunburned face. She starts walking out the door and around to the side of the house.

Like any other younger sister, Carrie is never far behind me. She doesn't like to baby-sit our sisters and she's never asked to. I'm the oldest. I'm the one stuck home babysitting all three of them. Carrie is the tattletale of the family.

I even have to baby-sit Mom when she gets *those feelings*. I have to give up my time to make sure she's not alone with Sam, now nine months old. She's afraid of hurting her. Carrie doesn't know how lucky she is to have her freedom.

"Wait! Come here!" I scream, afraid she'll notice my bag lying on the ground. That's all the ammunition she'd need to destroy what's left of me. "Watch the girls for a minute while I go smoke a cigarette outside. I'll give you anything you want from my room."

"Okay," she agrees.

It is that easy. We have been so conditioned to compensation in our house. Everything has its price here. I pay with my innocence. I think back to the cost of being his child.

"Dad, can we watch *Wizard of Oz* tonight? It comes on at seven o'clock."

"If you give me a butt massage for ten minutes." Dad bid the minutes like an auctioneer. He always started high. Sometimes I could talk him down in minutes and sometimes not. We could go back and forth deciding how long I would have to massage him. I wanted to do it as little as possible. Sometimes it was his butt, sometimes he would roll over. I'd have to squeeze his "legs."

Different requests had different price tags. Drinking the last of the milk was big. None of us kids were allowed to drink the milk if it was almost gone. If we wanted to play with friends, that cost too.

As much as I hated the butt massage, I hated the foot rubs just as much. He rarely bathed—which made him all the more repulsive.

His long toenails were only cut when Mom cut them. He never let me wash my hands after squeezing. To wash after touching him made him feel dirty and he despised that. Sometimes we'd go straight from a massage to the dinner table, and the smell—or maybe it was just the thought of what my hands had done—was nauseating. No matter what, the end was always the same. We paid for whatever we got and we had to abide by his price tags. Nothing was ever half price or on sale. It was his way or no way.

We had a small bathroom off the kitchen that was occupied by only a toilet. Dad didn't mind me using it—since there wasn't a sink, he wasn't worried about me washing my hands. I just rinsed my hands in the toilet bowl. I couldn't use the water in the tank for fear he would hear me taking the cover off. I dried off with the white sheets of paper and felt some gratification.

Dad's full head of straight brown hair was rarely combed. It was greasy and always full of sawdust. His torn wardrobe was also covered in wood shavings and varnish spots. He smelled of the cigarettes he was always smoking. He was a man I wished were dead.

I didn't know how much more he wanted. I wanted my hands to be my own to decide what they touched. I liked the feeling of my hands gripping the handlebars of my bicycle. I liked the way my body felt when I was in control of it—running free during track practice. I didn't like the intense fear in my hands when Dad was around. I had given him fourteen years of submission. Enough was enough.

CHAPTER 2

*"But if any provide not for his own, and
specially for those of his own house, he hath
denied the faith, and is worse than an infidel."*
1 Timothy 5:8

It is dark now and I take the trail next to the river by my house, the same river I tried to sail away in my inflatable raft a couple of weeks before. I bought it at a garage sale for fifteen dollars, using all of the baby-sitting money I had earned from Mom and Dad's friends. I had been swimming in this river before but never really explored it. I thought it would secretly carry me away to another town. That afternoon I had blown up the raft at the gas station, and once I was by the river, I loaded in my backpack and my cassette player/radio carefully wrapped in a black garbage bag. When in the water, I turned on my favorite Bon Jovi music and began to float. After about ten minutes, the creek widened to about fifteen feet, the current picked up, and I could tell the water was getting deeper. I looked to my right and saw something moving swiftly towards me. The black water snake made me question my plan. I could imagine it popping a hole in my boat with its fangs. I was terrified I would drown and be eaten up. I didn't have a choice. I had to go back. It was the last thing in the world I wanted to do.

As I stand by this river again, paranoia grips my soul. I'm terrified that Dad is hiding behind a tree and knows of my plan, although I don't think he could even imagine that I have it in me. His hold is so tight and the fear so strong.

I run and run until my breath has left me. My heart racing, I land on my older cousin Diana's porch. She's the only relative who lives in our town and I trust her.

"Let me in. My Dad's not here, is he?" I don't expect him to be but want to make sure.

"No, come in."

Mom and Dad are only a couple blocks away cleaning a restaurant for extra cash under the table to supplement their welfare checks. Diana was surprised to see me. I couldn't talk to her fast enough. "It's an emergency. *Do not* tell anyone that I am here."

"Okay, is something wrong?" I walk through her duplex, closing her drapes. I feel somewhat safe. I'm no stranger to moving and being on the run. I learned from the best.

The summer of 1983 we were driving in our brown van that was missing a back door. A piece of plywood in the door's place was all there was to keep the boxes from falling out. With the two dogs, three kids, and the stench of his cigarette smoke, it was almost impossible to breathe. The back windows didn't open and so we were left to inhale his rot. At one point the vehicle must have been used to haul things, because the seat that was in the middle row didn't match the front seats. We didn't have any seat belts, not that we would have wore them.

Sometimes we spent months on the road, bumming churches along the way for money, gas, and food. I passed the time in the small amount of space that remained in the back of the van next to the boxes and the dogs. I crouched down on the floor to try to have some sort of privacy. Any bump or jostle sent the piece of wood in the back into a fierce rumbling as if it was trying to escape its position. Frightened that at any moment I could tumble out of the enormous cavity that would be left in the event that it succeeded, I braced myself close enough to the middle seat to grab a last-minute hold if needed. I scribbled in my journal about growing up and having children. It gave me peace.

I was never allowed to discuss growing up with my parents. I wondered how many children I would have. Where would I live? Who would I marry? Nothing could ever be wondered aloud, though. Mom and Dad were convinced the world would end and

Jesus would come again before I would ever grow up. They tried to convince Carrie and me that we would never have a life beyond the childhood they created for us. But they couldn't stop me from believing and they couldn't stop me from praying in secret. I'd pray partly because I was scared they were right, terrified of what would happen if I didn't and partly because of the true sense of love and understanding I felt from a father in heaven.

My journal gave me some peace from the chaotic rat race of the life they had chosen for us. I felt hope about a future they said wouldn't come. I knew that one day I would have my own children and my own family. We would be happy.

Crossing the country, whether it be hitchhiking or driving, was something we've done many times. When things got rough or Mom and Dad got bored we ran. We ran until they tired.

Mom sat in the front seat with her third daughter – four year old Bree – on her lap. I asked, "Where are we going this time?" Immediately I realized what a futile question I was asking. But for once I prayed we would actually have a destination. But we didn't. I was not surprised but nonetheless I was disappointed. I thought to myself, *When I have my own children, we will never be homeless. We will always have food to eat. They will always know where home is and it won't be a license plate number.*

It was the uncertainty in my life as it was that pained me the most. I especially disliked it when we moved away and were immediately out of money. That meant we didn't travel very far before stopping at any church we could find. Sometimes this meant only getting a couple hundred miles before the end of the day.

"Bummin' churches." That's the nickname I came up with for how we made our living. It was Dad's idea. Carrie and I had the job of steeple hunting. When we would notice a steeple or a church, we would yell out to Dad and he would maneuver the van in that direction. We became very good at it too. In large cities, like Hollywood, it could take us a long time to find our way to a steeple we had earlier spotted. I am certain we missed a few, but I doubt we missed very many. We knew the more we found, the more chances we had of getting a meal, gas, and ultimately a place to stay for the night. That was always my goal, to get out of the vehicle. I would get carsick from being in there for months at a time, stopping only to bum a church, eat, or sleep. We would stop at the churches during the daylight hours when someone was more likely to be there. If a building had its lights on, though, it wasn't safe from our begging. We'd hit every church, in every town, even stopping at churches within a block or just across the street from each other.

Occasionally Dad would go in by himself, ask for a pastor, priest, or minister, and prey on their pity to feed us and give us money. Sometimes he had over a hundred dollars from other churches in his pocket. He wouldn't spend it, though .Our bellies would be aching and roaring but he would hold out for some other church to feed us so he wouldn't have to spend the cash. If that didn't work out, we would pass from one mom-and-pop restaurant to the other asking the owners if they could spare some food for our family. We were always made to go in the restaurant and stand by Dad as he talked to the person in charge. All the customers would stare at us and listen to my father tell our sob story. The patrons didn't have to eavesdrop because Dad was quite loud and if an establishment refused to feed us, he wanted everyone to know.

Usually people were kind and compassionate. Once at a café, the owners said they would feed us lunch, but it would have to be a meal of their choice. We didn't know what to say when the waitress brought out five bowls of clam chowder. Dad said it was against the law of Moses to eat clams. So he took the sins upon himself when the waitress turned her back. He ate all five bowls of soup. We then had to lie to the waitress and tell her how good the lunch was.

He did take us out for McDonald's after that. If all else failed, he would spend some of the money to feed us. We definitely saw his anger in having to do so. He would bargain with us and say things like, "Okay, we can stop for the day, but tomorrow we have to work even harder to make up for the money we lost."

He deceived the clergy by telling them we had a destination and had run out of money for gas. If it were Sunday, we'd attend a service at a church and then meet with the pastor or priest to beg for money. Sometimes Carrie and I would get out of the vehicle and rub dirt on our faces. We tried to look as pitiful as possible. Dad claimed the religion of whatever church we were in that day, all the time making us fully aware that those churches were an abomination. He had taught us that one religion in particular worshiped statues and that we were never to do that. Yet while attending church meetings at a place that practiced it, he made us follow along, bowing down to statues. I thought Carrie and I were literally going to burn in hell for the things we were made to do. As I knelt at the altar I could feel Dad's gaze. It was a look that told me that this worshiping had better be just an act.

At times churches would offer us things other than money. They had vouchers for food and gas, for instance. Dad preferred the money so he could buy his cigarettes. The way he saw it was they just wanted to control his choices, which, of course, was the truth. Churches don't want people spending their congregations' tithing on cigarettes or booze.

Sometimes we were fortunate enough to get a room for the night. We begged at small mom-and-pop motels for a room. Dad would arrange where everyone slept.

"Kelly, you sleep between the beds on the floor," he said when Mom wasn't looking. He slept at the edge of his bed closest to me so he could hang his arm down in the middle of the night and rub his nasty hands all over my body. After a few times of that happening, I tried to never be alone with him before we got a room. That way he couldn't say I was disobeying. He couldn't tell me where to sleep. I slept in closets if I could. I tried to avoid being in his path to the bathroom so he couldn't touch me on his way for a midnight pee.

I would get my period on the road and there would be no money for maxi pads. Dad would hand me a cigarette filter. "Plug your hole with this," he'd tell me.

Once I had to have a bowel movement and there wasn't a bathroom around. Mom handed me one of our cooking pots. I pooped in the pan behind the middle seat of the van and then dumped the waste on the side of the road. Later that evening we stopped at a park to eat. Mom warmed some spaghettiOs over a fire. My hunger left me instantly when I saw what our meal was cooking in. There was that pot. Everyone was getting ready to eat out of it. I was told it had been washed, but the idea of it grossed me out nonetheless. Dad ate out of the pot without any problem, and I think he got some gratification from the fact that earlier I had been sitting on it. He was angry with me for even worrying about it. He felt low when I disagreed with him about anything.

CHAPTER 3

"But when the comforter is come, whom I will send
unto you from the Father, even the spirit of truth,
which proceedeth from the Father,
he shall testify of me."
John 15:26

"Yes, something is wrong. It's my dad, he won't leave me alone," I tell my cousin. There, I said it.

"Is he hurting you?" In her beautiful brown eyes, I can see an understanding starting to develop.

"Yes. I don't want to talk about it anymore. Are you gonna help me or not? If not, I need to leave and get a ride out of town."

"I'll do whatever you need me to do," she says and her soft-spoken voice comforts me.

"Good. I need to call my boyfriend."

Travis answers the phone, "Hello."

"Hi. Is it all right if I come over to your house tonight? I know it's late. I probably won't be able to get there until about twelve thirty."

"Sure come on over... Is everything all right? How are you getting out of the house so late?"

"I'll talk to you when I get there."

"Okay. My friend Tony is spending the night tonight. We'll take our sleeping bags and camp out on the front porch. That way my mom won't find out."

"See ya in a little while," I comment in a hurry. I stand in Diana's kitchen feeling like the walls are falling and Dad could hear and see everything I was doing.

"Bye."

"Bye."

I hide behind her furniture so that Dad won't be able to see me if he peers in through a crack in the curtains. I know he is going to come for me, but I don't know when .We don't have a phone, so they won't notice I'm gone until they come home from work— unless Carrie got brave and went to use a neighbor's phone to call the restaurant. I know it won't be long until my parents find me.

I run upstairs searching for a really dependable place to hide. I see the clothes dryer in the bathroom and wonder if I can fit in it. I am so convinced that Dad will come and search his niece's apartment. I just know it. I know her house will be the first place he'll check. I thought I would be out of town before he got home, but Diana can't take me right now. I have to wait until her two children fall asleep. She can take me then. Surely he would never suspect me to be hiding in the dryer.

"I have to test it before he gets here in case I don't fit in." The gravity of the situation gave way to some laughter as I crammed myself into the space. I barely fit.

She knows I'm scared. Does she know how much?

There is a knock at Diana's door. My insides twist up and choke the air out of me. Everything is a blur.

Now is the time.

"Hi, Uncle Paul."

"Hi. Have you seen Kelly?" His voice is a sickness that penetrates all of my senses.

I climb back into the tight space of the drier. I'm reminded of that dark suffocating feeling in the old refrigerator Carrie and I use to play in and how once I couldn't get out. I just want to get out of this dryer. I hear the evil in his voice as he hunts me down like a muskrat or raccoon he likes to trap.

"Well, if you see her, tell her to get her ass home."

He leaves.

Could it really be that easy? He gave up a lot quicker than I imagined. He didn't want to search her house.

He must be lurking around outside, snooping in the windows, I'm sure of it.

Diana comes up stairs and helps me out, one limb at a time.

"Did you lock the door?" I ask, worried.

"No... He won't come in without knocking."

"Please, please," I beg.

I wait upstairs for her to check the front door.

"It's okay now, Kelly. You can come down," Diana yells up the stairs.

Why is she so loud? Doesn't she know how sneaky he is?

Well I do. I have fourteen years of experience living with this pervert and I know all his tricks. At least I think I do.

Nine months earlier my beautiful baby sister, Sam, came into the world. The night she was born was also the perfect opportunity for Dad to get me alone. He left Carrie and Bree at home and walked me downtown to the bar. He said my friends could come over to our house if I would sit at the bar with him for a while.

"Pretend you're my girlfriend," he suggested as we walked up to the bar door. We entered and the smell of alcohol and cigarettes hung heavy in the room. It wasn't the first time I had been in a bar, but this was the first time I was supposed to act like an adult. I didn't want to be there, but I knew I didn't want to be home alone with Dad that night. This was the only way I could get him to let my friends come over. I hoped I could get one of them to spend the night.

"Is that your daughter?" somebody from the bar asked.

"Yes," I replied before Dad could say anything else. I could see his anger and it hung like a noose around my neck that kept getting tighter and tighter.

"I'll take one rum and coke and one regular coke," Dad told the bartender. While he was serving up the drinks, Dad pointed for me to sit in the booth furthest away from the bar. Once he was sitting in the booth with me, he switched the drinks. He kept the drinks coming. I didn't like the taste—it was sweet and made me full. I had to drink them, though. His overbearing presence scared me. He was in a hurry, too, so I had to drink fast. I was drunk for the very first time in my life.

I staggered back to the house with him, where he had a bottle of cherry brandy waiting for my friends and me. My friend Lori was a year younger than me and her brother Paul three years older. I had a crush on Paul and Dad knew it. We sat around playing some of Dad's drinking games, which mostly consisted of, "Here, Kelly, have another."

Then we played one of our favorite family games—"hide and seek" in the dark. While hiding, I was hoping Paul would find me, hoping he would kiss me. He didn't find me hiding in my room, but Dad did. He tried to pretend he was Paul, and pushing his body against mine in the dark, he copped a feel of my breasts. But Paul didn't smell of cigarettes and stale body odor, and Paul had never touched me before. I ran to home base, which was the couch downstairs, to try to stop any further touching.

When my friends left, I went to my room. I knew enough to push my bed against the door to try to keep Dad out. Mom was in the hospital. She had just given birth to their fourth girl. I had never been alone with Dad all night before. He was irate that the door was blocked. He started pushing and demanding that I move the bed. He didn't have to yell. His presence was enough.

Once in the room, his imperatives were law. I hadn't yielded to his "invitation" to sleep with him that night, so he invited himself to *my* bed. He slithered next to me.

Can I hold it together long enough to protect myself? I thought. The alcohol must have taken full hold and I passed out. I didn't remember another thing.

In the morning I felt terrible, and all I wanted to do was sleep and forget about the night before. My resilience gave way to hunger, though, and I had to go downstairs to get something to eat.

"You must not have minded me being in your bed last night. You let me squeeze your tits," Dad said and grinned like he knew something I didn't.

"When I went to stick my hands down your pants, you pushed them away," he remarked with a sly grin.

I didn't know what to say, so I didn't say anything. I didn't want to believe him. Did I really let him do that? I wished for Mom to be home.

CHAPTER 4

"None of you shall approach to any that is near of kin
to him, to uncover their nakedness: I am the Lord."
Leviticus 18:6

Diana says she'll drive me the thirty miles to Travis's house now. It's late, about midnight. As we walk to her car, I'm frightened Dad is lurking in the bushes. I make her start the car and then walk around her house to make sure Dad isn't around. She pulls over right outside the town of Arcade where Travis lives.

"Here, why don't you drive for a while?"

"Cool!" I say, surprised at the trust she has in me.

"Just keep to the speed limit."

"No problem," I say with a hint of freedom in my voice.

We arrive safely on Travis's dimly lit street. I feel safe in the dark. I made it. I open the car door cautiously, in case we were followed. As Travis walks down the front steps, I ponder what would happen if he knew why I was really there.

"Hi Travis. Diana wants to talk to you for a minute in the car." I am wondering what she will tell him, but I must trust in her that she won't tell him my secret. So I get out and he gets in.

After only a few minutes, he emerges from the vehicle. I hug her, she tells me she loves me and leaves.

"What did she say to you?" I ask as we walk down the sidewalk to obtain some privacy from Tony, who is now standing on the porch.

"She is worried about you and your problems at home. She says you can't stay there tonight."

"Well, I'm running away."

"Where will you go? How will you take care of yourself?"

"I dunno. I'll find a way."

"Maybe you can spend the night here with me. I'll wake up my mom and ask her. I'll just tell her it's an emergency and you need a place to stay."

"You don't think she will take me home, do you?"

"No, she has to work in the morning."

"Okay." My heart is pounding. Spend the night with a boy. Not just any boy, the boy of my dreams. I'm game.

He goes upstairs and talks to his mom. She says I can sleep on the couch as long as Travis isn't in the same room. That's okay with me.

We aren't sleeping yet, though, instead we are out on the front porch huddled together in his sleeping bag. Tony lays only a few feet away while Travis and I talk about having sex. I am willing, but Travis decides that since we are both virgins, we will wait. Sex is a big step that I am ready to take, but he isn't. So we kiss and kiss until I feel my lips are going to fall off. Finally we decide that I should go inside and sleep.

At fourteen, I was consumed with my social life. I spent Sunday afternoons skating at the roller skating rink down the street from my house. I lived for Sundays, especially after I met my first love, Travis. I remember how he looked when I first saw him. He wore name-brand jeans and expensive shoes. His blue-green eyes were so beautiful. I would only show his eyes the parts of me I wanted them to see.

Every week I walked to the rink with my friends. On each side of the square-enclosed floor was a row of long benches with carpeted seating areas that faced inward to watch the skaters. Tall panels of different colors stretched to the ceiling and separated the benches into booths. If anyone were tired all we had to do was take a rest on one of those carpeted benches. There were six booths on each side. In the back of the rink was booth six, the "kissing booth." It was always darker back there, so it was the perfect place for making out. The roller rink chaperones were older teenagers who would skate around and play games with us like limbo and pick-up skate. If they saw any funny business going

on in booth six, they would go over and shoo the sweethearts out
of there. I envied those who got to sit there. To me it was much
more than a make-out station. If you made it to booth six, it meant
someone cared for you, somebody wanted to be alone with you,
and everyone knew it.

The "pick-up skate" was a game we played every single Sunday.
It was both a blessing and a curse. Soft love songs would begin
to play and a couple would start the game by holding hands and
skating around. When the chaperone blew his whistle, the skating
girl would pick a new partner from those sitting on the booths to
the left and the boy would choose a new girl from those in booths
to the right. Song after song would play until almost everyone had
been picked. Of course there were the times that nobody would
pick me. Sometimes I would get lucky and find a little boy who
would accept my bribe. He would then choose me when it was his
turn. That way I had a chance to pick one of the many cute boys
that were there. The downside was that you could be rejected not
only by one boy, but also by a whole section of boys. It happened.
It happened to me and it happened to my friends.

The minute I woke up on Sunday, I would begin preparing
for the 2:00 p.m. opening of the skating rink. I started the day
listening to the weekly top 40 countdown with Casey Kasem. I
waited for the songs I loved to sing and taped them on my cassette
recorder. About noon I would walk over to my friend Lori's house
to take a shower. Only she and her brother Paul would be home,
so I could spend the next two hours in front of the mirror doing
hair and makeup.

The first thing I would look for when we moved into a place
was the same thing Dad would, the bathroom. Most of the places
we would rent weren't updated enough to have a shower. We were
lucky if the door shut completely. It never mattered though; he
always found a way to spy on me when I was naked, whether it
was slats in the door, keyholes that were too large, or bathroom
doors with windows in them. Any attempt at covering the open
areas sent him into a rage.

There was nothing I could say that would please him. He would
make me take the toilet paper out of the keyhole or the curtain
off the window. He insisted he wasn't looking. I learned not to

defend myself in these instances. I was not allowed an opinion unless it coincided with his.

Every bathroom in any place we lived had a revolving door. It never seemed to stay closed when I was in there. I could time Dad's bathroom breaks by when I took my bath. It seemed the running water stimulated his bowels. I would sit very still as to not disturb the washcloth that covered my lap. It was all I had to hide my shame. I would hold my arms tight across my chest to hide my breasts. The water would become cold and my body numb waiting for him to leave.

"Are you just gonna sit there? Aren't you gonna take a bath?" he would question as he covered his face with one hand. "I won't peek." He'd then continue spreading his fingers apart so he could see. Then he'd laugh.

"Yeah," I'd say, thinking, *That's what I was trying to do before you came in here.*

But I could never say such a thing to him.

When I'd think he was finished, he'd expose his genitals to me while standing and slowly pulling up his pants. He never wore underwear.

"Oh, I guess I didn't have to go after all," he'd say.

Sometimes it wasn't even five minutes before he was back. I learned to bathe quickly and in my swimsuit. The problem remained, though. He was always around. He had nothing else to do. All the baths in the world couldn't wash away the dirty feeling I got when he was in there.

"Why do you take a bath in your swimsuit?"

"I don't know."

"Do you think I'm going to look at you?" His anger was obvious but he never made me take it off. He thought teasing me about it and trying to make me feel stupid for doing it would make me stop. I knew better.

While I stood under Lori's shower, I would try to wash away the shame and humiliation I felt at home. I tried to rid my mind of the memories of other bathrooms and showers that were so unsafe and never private. Bathing at Lori's on Sundays was a Godsend. Little did I know I would meet an angel one Sunday at the rink.

Travis was apparently interested in my friend Tammy. They had been meeting at the rink and sitting in booth six together. I hadn't heard the gossip because I had been grounded for the past two weekends. I was totally out of touch with my social life and had missed all the cute boys. I was ecstatic while getting ready. I couldn't wait to hear the music, see my friends, and just be a teenager.

That's when I saw Travis for the first time. His nice clothes and body immediately caught my eye. Who was this boy? I had never seen him at the rink before. When I met him, I fell in love instantly. He was skating around the rink with a friend who was new too. He had nice jeans that showed his perfect behind, perfectly cut short brown hair, and the most mesmerizing blue-green eyes I had ever looked into. I asked my friend about him and she skated over to talk to him.

"Hey Travis, did you know that Tammy is grounded this weekend? She wanted me to tell you. By the way, have you met my friend, Kelly?"

Then, on cue I skated up beside him. Our introduction was perfectly executed. I knew he was interested in me when he asked me to skate with him. I was so nervous and worried about my sweaty hands that he would soon be touching.

He was handsome and taller than me, but not too tall. I was instantly impressed with his skating. That was a big deal because I would never be seen with someone who couldn't stand up on four wheels. We skated around the rink and he told me I was pretty. He seemed so mature; he came to the rink with his friends in their own car. He was so cool. All the girls liked him, and because of that, I was the recipient of a lot of angry teenage threats.

Travis and I would meet every Sunday. We skated and sat in booth six. We would kiss. We would kiss a lot. I couldn't get enough of him. We would meet our friends there and we always had a lot of fun. Roller-skating was the very best part of my life. I finally knew I wouldn't be left out of the pick-up skate. More importantly, I had made my way to booth six. I had arrived.

CHAPTER 5

*"Be not overcome of evil, but
overcome evil with good."*
Romans 12:21

The aroma of the French toast Travis's mom is making awakens my senses. The warmth of the blanket that covers me camouflages the reality of what I have done, but only for a moment. I jump to my feet and hurry to the window in the dining room. How long do I have before Dad finds me? I thought once I'd escaped I would feel safe, but now I am more afraid than ever. I am terrified. After breakfast, I ask to take a shower. I relax for a moment while the water rushes over my head. There is a knock at the bathroom door.

"Your Dad's downstairs," Travis says nervously.

I turn off the water and grab the closest towel I can find. Wrapped tightly in this temporary shelter, I peek out the window. Dad is standing in the driveway. He must have borrowed his friend Gary's car to come get me, because we don't own a car. He must have also borrowed Gary's twelve-year-old daughter, Chrissy. He has her squeezed tightly against his hip with her hand grasped in his.

Gary, Chrissy, and Chrissy's mom, Ginger, lived a few blocks from us down a dead-end street. You could feel the evil emanating from their house whenever we would go there. It was a big house with a big yard. The main floor was no longer used because it cost too much to heat. An old camper was parked in the back. I used to play with Chrissy in it on the days we got along with each other. I don't like her much ever since Dad gave her my brand-new jacket last winter. It was a beautiful pink coat and Chrissy wanted it. For some reason, Dad gave it to her. I wonder how he made her pay for it. After a week, it was nothing but a stained rag from her throwing it on the floor.

Their family had a pool that was about four foot deep and six feet wide. The pool was never cleaned and the water had long since turned into a four-foot deep slime pond. A pretty shade of green film lay over the top. Gary bathed once every year—he was very proud of that fact. The day he bathed was one we all witnessed. He put on some shorts, got into the pool, and sat there for thirty minutes. He then figured he was good for another year. I never liked going over there — the feeling I got was beyond creepy. It didn't help that Mom and Dad told stories of how the house was haunted and that was the real reason for Gary moving everything upstairs. He didn't even have a bathroom door, only a curtain that barely covered the hole in the wall. The entire upstairs was no bigger than the average living room; Gary partitioned it off into little sections. There was no running water up there either.

Gary loved his cat .One day our family was upstairs and there was this white sticky stuff all over the cat and the bed. Gary told us it was mayonnaise but Dad made sure he told me that it was from Gary having sex with his cat. *How can you have sex with your cat?* I thought. *What a sicko, why are we friends with this guy?*

The evil in our house was just as present. I slept in the pitch dark because I didn't want to see it. Mom felt it too. She's had feelings about stabbing the baby, ever since she brought her home from the hospital. The evil was all around us and there was no escaping its influence. She said there was a demon in our house working her to commit murder. It told her to kill her baby every minute of every day. The thoughts scared her so much. The voices told her they would not stop until she went through with it. She'd make me stay home if Dad wasn't around. She couldn't trust herself alone. Either Dad or I had to be home to stop her if she couldn't fight the voices anymore. She emptied the house of any sharp knives and left only butter knives in the drawer. I was worried for her and worried for Sam. If something happened to Mom, I would be left alone with Dad to be his new wife. There would be no one to stop him.

I look out the bathroom window at Travis's and ask myself, "Why did Dad drag Chrissy into this?! It's none of her business. Is it?" Frantically I pull my clothes out of my backpack and put them on. I must hurry before he has to have one of his "bowel movements" right here and now.

The conflict of emotions comes rushing at me like a tidal wave. *Why can't he leave me alone?* I don't want to get him in trouble. But I don't want to go home.

"I'm not going downstairs!" I tell Travis through the door.

"You have to go downstairs," Travis's mother gently coaxes, and I open the door. Her eyes are full of confusion and helplessness.

"I'm not going!"

"Kelly, if you don't come down, we'll have to call the police," Travis's sister, Danielle, calls from the landing on the stairs.

"I don't care. I can't do it. I can't come down." Travis's mother is looking at me carefully. She doesn't know what to do. Every thirty seconds I snatch a glance out the window to the driveway to make sure Dad hasn't come any closer to the entry.

Travis comes in and out of the bathroom like a reporter. "The police are here."

"Where's my dad? I don't see him in the driveway."

"He's in the dining room with the police." My heart sinks. The walls close in. I shake.

"If he'll leave, I'll come downstairs."

"Kelly, if you don't come down, the police will come up and make you come down," Travis's mom says.

I looked at Travis and took a deep breath. "Okay. See if they can make Dad go outside," I whisper to him. My heart pounding, I descend the never-ending staircase.

I go down the first five steps then stop to look at the window on the landing. I wish I could just fly through it. I force my feet to turn, knowing what waits at the bottom. I don't want to face him—his look would devour me with guilt. I look at my feet the rest of the way down to avoid looking at him.

By this time, everyone is in the dining room. "If you come home, you won't be in trouble," Dad says. But what he really means is, *Keep your mouth shut.*

"I am not going with him," I insist quietly, looking only at the police.

"Why did you run away? Why don't you want to go home?" they question.

"I just don't want to."

"Are you afraid to go home?"

"Yes."

"Are you afraid of what will happen to you because you ran away?"

"No."

"Did he hurt you?"

"Not exactly. Can't you make him go outside?" I plead.

"Did somebody hurt you?" I can feel Dad's fear swooping in over me and the power I have now. I don't like this feeling. I beg again for the officer to send Dad outside. After what seems like forever, he sends him out.

My guard is lifted but only just enough to get the words out. The officers' impatient gaze isn't making it any easier to say. I take a deep breath.

"Yes."

Outside an officer briefly questions Dad about Chrissy, who she is, and what she is doing with him. I wonder what kind of excuse he gave to justify the awkwardness.

He will have to slither over to the police station to respond to the complaint. I have to go to the police station too.

Danielle offers to hang with me for the day. It's Independence Day and Wyoming county is beaming with excitement. One of the Fourth of July events include a fair. Last night Danielle and I had made plans to go there together, now the only place I will be going is to visit local law enforcement.

Dad asks the police if he can first pick up my mom from work and take Chrissy home. He gets the police to agree. Now he can rid himself of the implication that Chrissy's presence might suggest. Thank goodness Dad's leaving.

"Can I just bring Kelly over to the station in my own car?" Danielle asks.

Danielle and I figure we have an hour. She agrees to lend support by staying with me as long as I need her to.

I should've known he'd find me. All he had to do was look up Travis's address in the phone book. When I first fell in love, I found a strength I didn't know I had. But when Dad found out from my tattletale sister, it became a weakness I couldn't afford. He turned that wonderful state of euphoria into a paranoid, no-holds-barred battle of the wills. He'd ground me from skating for no apparent reason.

He'd let me baby-sit his friends' kids, though, because he needed the money for his cigarettes. So I did what I had to do. One Sunday Travis snuck over to where I was babysitting. I made sure the curtains were drawn so Dad couldn't peek through if he showed up. It was my first defiant act as a teenager. I felt empowered. Although terrified, I knew I couldn't wait another week to see this boy. We had been secretly meeting in his friend's car to kiss during skating. I didn't even know how to kiss, but I knew I wanted to learn and I knew I wanted him to be the teacher. This was the boy of my dreams. He was seventeen and so mature.

Travis gave me my first hit off a joint. I didn't see the big fascination with it. I knew it was wrong, but I would do anything for him. I thought we would last forever. I was a poet and so was he. He wrote a poem for me once. It was the first thing anyone had ever written to me, and I was speechless. It was beautiful.

Travis had one downfall—he had money. He had a phone, car, and food on the table. I was wearing borrowed clothes along with my borrowed self-esteem. He was so different from the people in my world. I never wanted him to see my home or meet my parents, so I kept my life a secret. I made excuses for the minor conveniences we were lacking at our house, like a telephone.

If I had some babysitting money that Dad didn't know about, I would take a bus to see Travis. We didn't have a car and I didn't want him to find that out, so I told him I took the bus because my parents had to work and I couldn't get a ride. It was spring. We had all the time in the world and every moment was spent thinking of the boy.

I met his mother for the first time one Saturday afternoon when she and Travis pulled up to the Franklinville bank in a red sports car. I was waiting there with my three-wheeler. We had been planning this little trip for about a week. I wanted to take him into the woods and just play and have fun. I had spent many hours in the woods alone riding the trails and making some new ones of my own. I didn't want him to see where I lived, so I asked him to meet me there.

"Aren't we gonna go to your house so I can meet your parents?" asked Travis.

"No, I thought we'd hit the trails right away, if that's okay."

"But I want to see where you live."

"Maybe another day." The truth was my parents knew he was meeting me and they knew we were going to go three wheeling. They didn't like the idea. But Dad liked anything he could use as leverage.

The three-wheeler had been purchased by Dad to use for trapping, but he let Carrie and I use it sometimes. I knew better than to drive it down the sidewalk, because I'd get a ticket from the police. It was not against the law, however, to push it on the sidewalk. It was a little difficult to push a three-wheeler a mile, though, so I would turn it on and give it small amounts of gas while standing alongside of it. When I was sure the coast was clear, I would get one foot up on the peg and gun it. If I saw the pigs (that's what Mom and Dad called the police), I would simply hop off.

Travis and I walked away from the bank and toward the elementary school. I had permission to ride along the school's property to get to the woods. As we turned, I saw two people that looked like they crawled out of a cardboard box heading our direction. They were pushing a baby carriage that must have been pulled from a dumpster forty years before.

My world began to crash. I couldn't believe my eyes. There they were. Their hair was unkempt, and their clothes were full of holes and too small. I wanted to cross the street and pretend I didn't know who they were, but that would only land me in the garage with my pants down for a spanking and Travis would be sent home. There were no turns between them and us, so a detour was out of the question. As we walked closer, I waited for Travis to say something about these weird-looking people. I prayed he wouldn't. I was so humiliated that these two were my relatives. He had no idea. We were just about to pass them on the sidewalk and I knew I had better stop and introduce them to him.

"Mom and Dad, this is Travis. Okay, see ya later," I said, hoping they wouldn't say anything.

Earlier in the day, they had been ranting on and on about what a jerk this boy must be because he didn't want to come to our house to meet them.

We walked on. Travis seemed shocked that I hadn't mentioned anything until we had almost passed them.

We headed for the woods and had a great time playing on the three-wheeler. I even let Travis drive a little. I loved holding onto his waist while we rode. We stopped at a pond that I liked to visit. It wasn't much to look at, but I wasn't looking at the pond. I was looking at him and wanting him to kiss me. He did. A few hours later we met his mom again in front of the same bank. I rode home on a cloud. My blue skies gave way to thunderstorms though. My Mom and Dad proceeded to tell me how they disliked "the boy" and how he must have felt that our house wasn't good enough for him to visit. Any act of defiance or any demonstrated strength would have to be counteracted with a dose of Dad's type of humbling, so I stayed quiet.

CHAPTER 6

*"The wolf also shall dwell with the lamb, and the
leopard shall lie down with the kid; and the calf and
the young lion and the fatling together; and a little
child shall lead them."*
Isaiah 11:6

The main street of Arcade, New York, basks in the July sunshine
and Danielle comforts me on the way to the police station. We pull
into the lot and an air of uneasiness and apprehension filters into
my thoughts. The secret is out.

Danielle turns off the car and places a hand on my shoulder.
"Everything is going to be okay, Kelly. Are you ready?"

I smoke a quick cigarette and open the door. I didn't want it to
come to this. We approach the door to the station from the east.
I'm worried about Mom. She is going to be so angry with me. But
she'll finally know why I left and surely forgive me. I hear some
talking to my left.

"Oh no." Mom and Dad are approaching the same door from
the west. Mom has no idea why Dad has brought her here. The
distance between us is closing. I walk with my eyes focused on
my destination, the door.

Mom had to leave work and get a babysitter. She can't afford
that. She had to borrow a car and probably money for gas. I know
she's angry and I feel sorry for her. It's another black mark to add
to the others Dad has scarred me with. I feel their fear and rage
cutting through the safety I felt only moments ago.

Mom looks at me expecting I will at least say something, but I can't and I walk on, more determined to reach the door before they do. I don't want to have to walk past them in the waiting room.

The angle narrows as the four of us close in on the door. I can smell fear competing with the control that has been taken from Dad. Mom looks so tired in her food-stained and wrinkled shirt. I step up the pace and enter the building. Mom and Dad are so close that they make it in before the door even closes behind me.

Inside the station, the daylight quickly gives way to a cold and gray room with a doctor's office style reception window. I get goose bumps from the air conditioner. I step up to the counter and inform the lady standing behind it of my name. She immediately escorts Danielle and me to a back room. Mom and Dad are left in the waiting room to stew in their anger.

Dad had always been my defender. I was six when we moved to Chaffee. The first thing that Dad did was send us girls to the new neighbors to borrow food, cigarettes, coffee, or toilet paper, as he always did upon our arrival to a new home. Upstairs lived a single mother and her two kids, Denise and Joe.

I was the same age as Joe and became friends starting fires under my back porch. One day we fought and I pushed him down the stairs. There was blood everywhere. He wasn't moving. His head had hit the sidewalk so hard. I tore down the steps and around the corner into my apartment and got Dad. He ran outside with me. The ambulance had been called and Dad was telling me not to say anything to anyone about pushing him. He told me to go back into the house, but I stayed outside and watched as the ambulance people tried to help Joe. I could see Dad arguing with the boy's mom. Joe would be okay, just a bad cut on his head.

Denise from upstairs used to baby-sit Carrie and me. She came over when Mom and Dad went to a jamboree or some other thing that they didn't want us kids to attend. Denise was the babysitter in charge, but I was the boss when she was not looking. Carrie and I were playing in the bathroom medicine cabinet when I found some nail polish remover. I had never smelled anything like it. I knew it was poison—there was a yellow "Mr. Yuck" sticker on its bottle.

I told Carrie to drink it. She wouldn't. After some convincing, she finally agreed to lick the piece of toilet paper that I had soaked in the acetone. I dumped the remaining liquid down the drain and ran to tell Denise that Carrie drank the entire bottle. Denise smelled Carrie's breath and called the ambulance. When they arrived, they induced vomiting right away. Gross! I didn't know they were gonna do that. They made her throw up right there on the kitchen floor. In a weird way, it was kind of funny. Carrie told them that I made her do it. After the chaos settled, I told Mom and Dad that she didn't really drink the whole bottle. Carrie didn't have to go to the hospital.

I took out my anger on my sister because I was bitter about all the attention Dad gave me and not her. Many of our problems were normal sibling rivalry, but they were compounded by the fact that everything around us was anything but normal.

Sometimes Mom and Dad had company over to play cards. Some of their friends had babies. I liked being the babysitter while the parents got drunk in the other room. Their babies were easy to control. I liked to hurt them and make them cry. They didn't seem like people to me. They were another thing to control.

When Carrie and I had our girlfriends over, we would kiss each other behind the doors of my room so nobody would see us. We would cut ourselves and mixed our blood together in a pact of sisterhood. We were "blood sisters." At seven years old, not many of my friends were allowed at my house. Those who did come over found it strange that Dad had me rubbing him in front of them. I began to wonder, *Is this normal? Do other families do this too?*

I began to feel weird about intimacy before I was even out of the first grade. At night I laid in bed thinking about controlling my friend Heather. Even though I didn't know how or why, I wanted to do to someone the things that were done to me. I almost did it. I came so close to sneaking out my window while everyone was asleep. My plan was to run to Heather's house and crawl in her window. I had unlocked her window earlier that day when we were listening to "Puff the Magic Dragon" and "Muppets" records in her bedroom. I knew the window would be easy to get into. I would then climb onto the bed and act out Dad's fantasies on someone else. I had planned to bring something to gag her with so her parents wouldn't wake up. Every detail was planned, but could I put my thoughts into action and go to a place in my mind I may never return from?

There was a deeper misgiving that kept me from acting on that impulse. I didn't want to lay a trap for my soul. I could never have accepted the way Dad wanted me to identify with him. There was a part of me that was fundamentally separate from Dad and his abyss.

CHAPTER 7

"For nothing is secret, that shall not be made manifest; neither anything hid, that shall not be known and come abroad."
Luke 8:17

The back room of the police station has no windows. It is occupied only by chairs, a table, and a refrigerator. Danielle and I sit at a wood table - the kind with metal folding legs - waiting for someone to come and tell what is going to happen. Our chairs are regular folding chairs with black vinyl that hold in the cold air from the room. Our short legs stick to the seats while we wait. It isn't long before a detective enters the room.

"Can I get you something to drink, ladies, before we get started?"

"Yeah, I'll take a pop, whatever you have is fine."

I think to myself, *Oh damn, now I have to tell this guy, who I don't even know, the most humiliating and hidden parts of my life.* I decide to only tell him a little. In fact, I have never told anyone all of it. I'll be damned if I'm going to be forced to tell a stranger the words I can't even bring myself to hear. *I have to vomit.*

July 4th 1986   1:45pm Arcade, New York

Statement of Kelly L. ------ as given to Det. Sgt. J. J. Clueless of the Cattaraugus County Sheriff's Department

Question: What is your full name and date of birth?

Answer: *Kelly Lynn ------, December 16, 1971.*

Question: *Where and with whom do you live?*
Answer: *Franklinville with my mom, dad, and three*
             sisters.

Question: *How old are your sisters?*
Answer: *Twelve years, seven years and nine months*

Question: *Can you tell me why you are here today?*
Answer: *Because I want it to stop, it isn't right.*

Question: *What do you want to stop?*
Answer: *I want my father to stop feeling places*
             he shouldn't—my breasts, my butt, and
             sometimes my pubic area.

Question: *How long has this been going on?*
Answer: *About two years.*

My mind wanders for a moment and I try and think back to when this all started. The beginning has long since vanished. But the moment Dad's sickness crossed yet another boundary was a night I can never make disappear.

We lived in a barn that was converted into a house. It sat back away from the street with another small house in front of it. The kitchen and living room were upstairs while the bedrooms were downstairs.

I was sick a lot and prone to ear infections and the flu. It could have been all the bugs that lived in the walls. They crawled all over the dishes. I told Mom and Dad, "Those aren't cockroaches, they are potato bugs!" It made me feel better to say that. Somehow "cockroaches" just sounded so dirty. Our house was clean. Mom always made sure of that. At night, Dad turned out the lights and waited patiently for the bugs to come out of hiding. After a few minutes, he would flip the lights on and begin the slaughter with his flyswatter. Hundreds of them came out of the woodwork. Each morning Mom cleaned up the dead bugs from the prior night's "hunt."

Dad had sold our bunk beds. He did that periodically when he needed money. People liked the beds he made. They have all the sturdiness and looks of a homemade piece of furniture. Since we remained bedless, Carrie and I slept on the couch, she on one end and myself on the other. Mom and Dad slept on a mattress on the floor and Bree was in her room. He had orchestrated where everyone would sleep that night and I would soon find out why. He would get angry when questioned and expected his orders followed without question. I obeyed and slept where he assigned me.

He had situated his mattress on the floor so that he was directly under the side of the couch where I slept.

As I fought for more room in my sleep, I sensed something creeping up my leg. I dismissed it quickly. "It must be Dad up to his old tricks," I thought. I soon realized that this was no prank. It was Dad's hand on my thigh. I laid still, petrified from fear.

Maybe he's dreaming, I thought. *Maybe he thinks I'm Mom.* Then his hand crawled uncomfortably close to my Wonder Woman panties. I realized that he was awake and that he knew exactly what he was doing, because he was not only touching my thigh now but also caressing it. He was getting closer and closer to my vagina. My heart was racing. I could hear it in my ears. It was deafening. I didn't know what was happening. Everything I knew to be true and real in life was destroyed in an instant, a tiny speck in time. My body lay frozen in denial for a moment but only for a moment. *I must do something quick.* But what? I pretended to change positions to dislodge his hold on my leg, but it didn't work. He was very determined and continued without hesitation. I decided showing him I was awake was my best defense.

"Oh Dad, did you want me to rub your feet?" I couldn't think of anything else to say. I knew that I had to pretend that nothing had happened. It was my only alternative. It was the middle of the night, he was my father, and I wasn't sure of anything anymore.

He answered, "Yes, I want you to rub my feet."

I'd do anything to make him stop. Until that night, he had never touched *me*. He had made me touch *him*, but never had he touched *me*. I got off the couch and began rubbing his nasty feet. Mom slept there next to him and never awoke. I was willing to keep rubbing all night to keep him from pursuing what he started. After about a half an hour, he let me go back to sleep. From that point on, nothing would be the same. This heavy feeling would never leave me. That one moment, that five minutes, had crumbled my entire eleven-year-old world.

I was blossoming into womanhood physically but was stifled emotionally by a person who thought of me only as an object. His object. My family was now different. Dad and I were different. We had a secret now.

The next morning I decided to forget. I would act like nothing had happened. I must have done something wrong to encourage this behavior. I knew that's what Mom would say if I told her. She had already accused me of being horny once when the family was wrestling on the floor and tickling each other. She said it in front of Dad.

"What, are you horny, Kelly?"

We engaged in tickling and wrestling often. This was nothing new. I was appalled that she would accuse me of such a thing. "Horny" was a dirty word they both used to describe each other. Now she was projecting that on me. It was hurtful, humiliating, and exactly the kind of thing I wouldn't want him to hear. Maybe he believed. Maybe it was my fault.

The night after Dad stuck his hand up my nightgown, he was watching *Something About Amelia* on TV. It was a movie about a girl who was sexually abused by her father figure. It was so uncomfortable to be in the same room with him when it was on. I held my bladder as I laid on a mattress until the movie was over. I didn't want him to see me watching it. I just wanted to forget. I was hoping he wasn't taking notes. I laid so still and pretended to sleep. But I was watching and peeking from under the covers. I was covered in sweat because my heart was beating so fast. But I didn't dare move.

Back in the police station, Detective Clueless continues to ask stupid questions.

Question:	*How often does it happen? When he feels you?*
Answer:	*Every day.*

Question:	*What does he usually do?*
Answer:	*He says I can have whatever I want if I listen to him. "Life will be easier," he says. I'll just be standing there and he will do it. I'll tell him to knock it off and he just laughs about it.*

Question:	*When you say "he will just do it," what do you mean?*
Answer:	*Just feel my breasts or my butt.*

Question:	*Does your father usually rub these spots or just pinch them?*
Answer:	*He grabs.*

Question:	*Does he just grab and let go?*
Answer:	*No he grabs and holds on.*

Question:	*Has there been any incidence where he grabs you under your clothes?*
Answer:	*Yes.*

Question:	*Do you remember when and what happened?*
Answer:	*I don't remember when, but it's usually on my breasts.*

Question:	*Has it ever been anywhere else besides your breasts?*
Answer:	*Yes, a few times he grabbed my bare butt.*

Punishments varied like the weather, but I could always count on Dad's sexual gratification being the outcome. His new thing was to take me to the garage for a spanking. Once while walking out the back door to the garage, I saw Mom watching us through the kitchen window but she didn't stop him. Once in the garage, he shut the door. Dad settled himself into a hardback wooden chair.

All I could do was wait for my spanking. That's what he called it anyway. I knew better. I would have much rather had a "whoopin" than one of his punishments. They could last for any number of minutes and since he never owned a watch, he controlled the time and made it start and stop at his leisure. He would get a disturbed look on his face. It was one I was familiar with. He would get it when the evil took over. His body language changed and almost every move he made from his head to his feet was filled with innuendo. He wouldn't look me in the eyes. I was his property and he thought of nothing but his pleasure and how he could get it.

I had pubic hair and breasts. Sometimes I had a maxi pad on. I didn't want to pull down my pants. "I'll be grounded for however long you say instead. Okay?"

"No. Just get over here and get it over with. Quit acting like it's going to kill you. I am your father." After pulling down my pants, he'd make me lay across his lap. A distorted grin would come across his face. His eyes seemed to roll back in his head. I tried not to lie on the erection I knew he had. He would position me where he wanted. He would accept nothing else but total control. He started by giving me a little slap. It didn't hurt. He had to make it look real. I don't know for whom, though, because we were alone. He continued squeezing my butt and followed with another little slap and some more squeezing. Mom remained in the kitchen, oblivious to anything but her own problems about the demon in our house that was trying to get her to kill my baby sister.

He was always extra nice to me after those episodes and it would be almost impossible for Mom to punish me because he wouldn't let her. I never liked the fact that my punishments weren't normal. There didn't seem to be an end to his madness. I was getting older and stronger emotionally. I knew I had to do something and soon. Dad's jealousy was ruining what life he allowed me to have. The mere mention of a boy's name enraged him—especially Travis's name.

It wasn't long before I was getting grounded for just about anything I said or did. He would do anything to keep control over me. When I would help Mom in the kitchen, he would come up behind me and grab my butt. I wondered why he didn't grab my mom's butt. She was his wife and she was standing next to me doing dishes. Since I wasn't allowed to show my disgust or dislike of what he did, I'd click my tongue. It was all I could do, but it only made things worse. He wanted absolute submission from me. He couldn't even walk by me without touching me in some sort of sexual way.

My body matured and so did the intensity of our arguments. They always ended the same, though, me grounded and in the garage with him. Then he'd unground me and fight with Mom.

Mom blamed me. He controlled my life and the way she viewed me. He kept her distanced from me emotionally by keeping her angry with me. Mom and Dad were constantly fighting about me and how she thought Dad was spoiling me.

My mind shifts back to the present.

Question: *Do you remember when that was?*
Answer: *Six months ago, maybe.*

Question: *Why didn't you tell someone sooner?*
Answer: *I thought it would stop and he said if I told, I would be in trouble.*

Question: *Do you feel as though your sisters are subjected to this same thing?*
Answer: *No.*

Question: *Where does all this usually happen?*
Answer: *My house.*

Question: *What kinds of things does your father say to you?*
Answer: *He says there is nothing wrong with it. Once during the past winter while my mom was gone a few days, he said I could come lie down with him during the night.*

Question: *Is there anything else you would like to add to this statement?*
Answer: *No.*

Question: *Is there any reason why you told somebody now about what went on?*

Answer-:   *Yesterday I asked him (my father) if I could go to my boyfriend's and he said, "Come over here and we'll talk about it." I said, "What do you want?" He said, "Sit down." Then he said, "Roll over and let me feel your butt." I said, "No that's stupid," and he answered, "It's not stupid."*

The questioning seems to take hours. Afterward I read everything I said and have to sign it. I skip through it at a glance; it's so many pages long. The last thing I want to do right now is take my mind through the turmoil of reading on paper everything I had just revealed. My statement is shorter - than the two hours it took him to write it and not everything is in my own words. Most everything I've said seems to be condensed into this detective's version. I sign it anyway. I just want this day to be over. I hadn't told him everything but I told him enough.

"I am going to need a list of friends that have been at your house and spent time with your dad," the detective demands. Does he really think that is necessary? Reluctantly, I give him Lori and Chrissy's names.

After the exhausting interview, Mom is brought in. She doesn't know why she's sitting here; Dad has left it up to me to break her heart.

"Allegedly your husband has been touching your daughter." Mom looks at me like I have just destroyed her very soul.

"You lying little bitch. Who's this girl and why is she getting in our business?" Mom states angrily, referring to Danielle sitting next to me.

"This is Travis's sister."

"Well, get her out of here!"

I knew this would happen and can feel Mom's sense of betrayal. The officer asks Danielle to leave. I feel embarrassed for Mom. I only wanted Danielle there for support. I realize this has made an already brutal day even more unbearable for her. I lack the strength to face everything on my own. Mom doesn't see it that way. I have crushed her.

Dad sits out in the waiting room unscathed.

CHAPTER 8

"And all thy children shall be taught of the Lord; and
great shall be the peace of thy children."
Isaiah 54:13

Trying to find a place for me to stay seems the next task of the day. I see myself getting stranded in the rush of events. I sit in that room while phone call after phone call is directed at potential foster families. It's the Fourth of July and people aren't home or they don't have room for another child. I wonder what will happen if they don't find a place for me to stay.

"Will I have to go home if you can't find a foster family?"

"You will not be going home," a chubby blond lady in her thirties reassuringly says as she places her hand on my shoulder. She works for social services. She has been called to make arrangements for me.

"If all else fails, you can stay here tonight," another policeman tries to set my mind at rest.

Thank God Detective Clueless's shift has ended. He revised my five-page statement to a mere 1 page interpretation of what I had actually told him.

After hours of searching, the news comes. There is a family that may be willing to take me in. I hear the caseworker talking to a foster parent.

"I don't care if she's a girl... There is no place for her to go tonight... Can't you just make an exception? Okay... I'll try a few other places."

"Why can't I just leave? I feel like everyone's lives are shifting to revolve around me. I don't want to be a burden." This is power thrust upon me. I don't want it. And I don't know what to do with it. I don't understand why I can't stay with Danielle.

Suddenly I hear the policeman on the phone.

"All right, I'll have the social worker get her some dinner before she brings her over... You will be home when? Okay... Yes. Only two days... We understand... Thank you so much for doing this. You really were our last hope."

I don't know which is louder, my pounding heart or my growling stomach. I'm so hungry. I haven't eaten since the French toast.

My "assigned" caseworker will be taking me to a foster family. She will be taking me away from the only family I have ever known. I will have new parents, new rules, and maybe even new brothers and sisters. I begin to feel a deep sadness about what I have done not only for myself but also for my entire family. I have a sense of hope, though. Now that I'm gone, maybe Mom can have her life the way she wants it—without me around. It saddens me to remember the good times and it makes me feel equally as guilty.

My parents weren't all bad. We shared some fun times, too. They took us camping all the time. We'd picnic, fish, and swim. We spent a lot of time with cousins and aunts and uncles. The summers were always full of family get-togethers. We never had any money but Mom and Dad were fun people when they wanted to be. At the family gatherings, Dad was always affectionate with the women who had married into the family. Everyone seemed to love him with his one hand on a beer and the other passing judgment on anyone who disagreed with him. He would preach, and they would listen. I often wondered how he did that. He could be so playful sometimes and that was the hard part. It was as if Dad had two personalities.

He was always pulling pranks on people, especially on company. When friends were over for dinner and Bible study, Dad would tie some fishing line to the rabbit ears that sat on the television set. Then he'd snake the line through the room to his chair. Nobody suspected a thing. Carrie and I waited with anticipation for him to play his joke. As we all sat in the living room, he'd give the line a tug. The rabbit ears would then slowly slide across the TV. You could sense the uneasiness in the room.

"What was that?" they would ask, as if something supernatural was occurring.

In unison our family replied, "I didn't see anything." It was comical watching the people as their fear grew and showed on their faces. Sometimes Dad would tell them it was a joke and sometimes he wouldn't. He got great joy out of playing tricks on people.

I have an uncle Ed who is a transvestite. He is married to my mom's half sister. We spent a lot of time visiting aunt Shirley when we were young, so we were exposed to uncle/aunt Ed's unusual dress. It made me laugh to see him answer the door in my aunt Shirley's pink bathrobe. He said he liked the way a woman's clothes felt on his body.

Dad decided to play a trick on his sister, my aunt Helen, one Halloween night. Uncle Ed was at our house and was dressed as a playboy bunny. He shaved his legs and had high heels on. His short brown hair was worn in a style a man or women could pull off. The black bow around his neck accentuated the v-neck black outfit he was wearing that he filled with a stuffed bra. The bright red lipstick made him look even more attractive. Nobody would ever take him for a man.

Dad sent him to Helen's house to pretend he was a woman interested in her husband. Dad thought it would get Aunt Helen's green-eyed monster roaring. I had to go with Ed to show him where Helen lived. I was dying to see what would happen. I hid around the corner of the building while Ed knocked on her door.

"Hello."

"Hi, is Mike here?" Mike was Helen's bedridden husband.

I couldn't stop laughing. Helen started to yell out to my dad, accusing him of this prank. It seems she knew her brother and his tricks all too well.

She didn't fall for it at all, but the rest of the town did. I escorted Uncle Ed that night to the fire hall's Halloween dance where he took first place for best costume. I've never seen so many men hit on someone before. He was asked to dance several times but always declined. Looking back, it was probably a good thing he did. While accepting his monetary award, he spoke in the microphone. His deep voice shocked the audience and the silence gave way to laughter. After the laughter came the anger—some men were really mad. I suppose they felt embarrassed about being attracted to him. I had to get him out of there before he got beat up.

Dad loved to play games and our house was perfect for it. He never cared what we did when we played. Our favorite game was hide and seek in the dark. The entire house and yard were included. There was a tree I would climb next to the garage. Once on top of the garage, I would take a leap to the back roof of the house and climb in the window. This was my secret weapon when I was about to be caught. I used it many times to escape from being IT. I can only imagine the way the neighbors saw us. We must have looked like animals. This game was usually a fun time for the family. It was fun for me until I started growing up and Dad would come and find me in the dark.

As if it wasn't enough that we kids were loud and obnoxious, Dad's loud too. He has spent his life making money his own way. Besides trapping, he enjoys creating things out of wood and selling them at auctions and craft shows. His favorite things to make are bunk beds. He cuts the boards, sands them down, drills, and then screws them together. He made them out in the front yard. When his tools weren't in the pawn shop and when we weren't on the road, the front of the house resembled more of a sawmill than a house. The furniture was nice but they didn't pay the bills. The state paid our bills. What they didn't pay, mom had to. She has always worked and does the best she can. At times both Mom and Dad would take jobs under the table to pay the bills. Dad avoided working at any cost. He'd rather not subject himself to being under authority, so he trapped muskrats and beavers. In the winter, he'd deer hunt.

I never saw Mom apply herself and become what I knew she had inside of her. I don't think she believed in herself anymore.

I looked at old photos and saw a girl who took pride in herself. Her hair was always done pretty and she always had jewelry on—not too much but just enough to add a sparkle to her look.

I thought she was beautiful. I loved my mother. I look at the photos of her with her first vehicle. She looked like a girl who was heading somewhere, a girl with a mission. Then she met him and everything changed. Years of being under Dad's control have taken a toll on her. I could see it even then.

CHAPTER 9

*"And thou shalt love the Lord thy God with all thine
heart, and with all thy soul, and with all thy might."*
Deuteronomy 6:5

On the way to the first foster home, the social worker takes me
to the county jail to eat dinner, served up by the prisoners. I walk
the line with my tray in hand. While making my way to the room
where it was decided I would eat, I see one of Dad's friends and
then another, dressed in orange, waiting for their dinner. They are
as surprised to see me as I am to see them. The social worker is
even more surprised that I actually know these people.

She asks me, "How do you know the prisoners?" I tell her
they are Dad's friends. I keep quiet about the fact that they buy
prescription drugs from Aunt Helen.

When I was eleven, I would always stop at my aunt Helen's
apartment on my way home from school. It was on the main street
not far from my elementary school. I could tell immediately if
she was home because she padlocked her door from the outside
if she was gone. Her husband, Uncle Mike, was bedridden and
she left him locked inside. Aunt Helen was always worried about
her neighbor girls. She thought they wanted to sneak in her
house to rape her husband. The neighbors were in their twenties
and I thought it was ridiculous that they would be interested in
a bedridden old man. My parents would laugh endlessly about
Helen's insecurities. I worried along with them for his safety. He
was trapped. If there were ever a fire in the building, he would
have no way to get out. The living room windows were about

shoulder height and I knew he could hardly get out of bed, let alone out a window. The window in his bedroom was boarded shut so nobody could get to Mike.

In the summer months, when I was on vacation from school, Helen would pay me to baby-sit Uncle Mike. She cleaned the bar across the street every morning for cash. I loved babysitting him. It got me out of my house and I had their apartment to myself. Mike never was any trouble; he just lay in bed and slept most of the time. She paid me with a bag of salt and vinegar chips and a glass of coke she poured from the bar. She had cable TV and that was the best part about babysitting there. More importantly, I didn't have to pay Dad to watch it. Inevitably, upon her return, the knocks at the door started. Aunt Helen would try to hide the pills she was selling, but I knew what she was doing.

At the police station, I get to eat in a room by myself away from the inmates. The food isn't half bad, considering. I can't believe I am eating in jail. The thought of what will happen to me is beyond terrifying. I had been in a jail only once before.

Once a week Mom and Dad had their Bible study classes. Sometimes it was at their friend Judy's house. I enjoyed it when I got to go and I believed every word I was taught about the Bible. I believed every interpretation Dad made. He was one of the smartest people I knew when it came to religion. I started to see contradictions, though, in what he preached and what he lived. He implied that allowances were made for people like him— people who were so close to the Lord, that is. Somehow his words smoothed over his deeply superficial conviction. Wow, could he get people to listen. The room was never large enough for anyone else's opinion. I sensed fear from some of the people. Nobody dared challenge Dad or his version of anything they read. What were they so afraid of? Gary and his wife Ginger often attended, along with some other couples. Judy, a single lady, frequently hosted. They all believed in Dad and shared his beliefs.

Mom and Judy were friends. She told Mom of her new boyfriend, Tony. His permanent address was "Attica State Prison." She wanted Mom to meet him.

"He's really religious."

"What's he in jail for?"

"Killing his wife... but he didn't do it," she added, somewhat defensively.

She believed in Tony and I had no reason not to. Judy somehow met him while he was in prison and started to write letters to him. She fell in love. Mom understood her dilemma. After all, her husband had been in jail before too, and look how he turned out. They made plans to meet him the next time Judy drove up there. It was a short drive from Judy's house.

"Can I go?" I asked. They both agreed it was a good idea. They wanted to convert him to our religion and an additional missionary was always welcomed.

We made plans for the weekend. It was so exciting. At twelve I had never been in a jail before. I wondered what I would say to this man. I felt awful that an innocent man would be living in a place like Attica.

I had heard many stories about Attica State Correctional Facility growing up. It's a maximum-security facility in upstate western New York. In 1971, approximately 1,300 prisoners led a riot against the prison and the guards demanding better living conditions and more opportunities for learning. Many people were killed during the four-day standoff. It was all over the news then and people still talked about it. John Lennon even wrote a song about it called "Attica State." He poetically sang about freedom, love, and peace, sympathizing with the prisoners.

As we entered the prison I heard the clatter of the metal gates. We were asked to empty our pockets onto a desk and leave our belongings there with the guard. Then we were checked with the metal detector. Once that was finished, we walked down a wide hallway and I saw a vending machine with my favorite snack, Twinkies. I stopped to look and Mom bought me a pack. What a treat! Another set of gates closed behind us as we entered a very large room with many guards standing around. To my left I saw a row of long tables lined up end to end. We were directed to sit at the end closest the exit. That's when I saw Tony. He had on his orange prison jumpsuit. I was so nervous. Tony, Judy, and Mom started to talk. I had no idea what to say when Judy introduced me, so I asked him if he wanted part of my Twinkie. He said, "No thanks." The entire time we sat there, I studied him and everything around me. When he started to talk to me, I asked him if he knew any of the other prisoners sitting on his side of the table.

"See that man next to me down at the end?"

"Yah."

"He's the guy who shot John Lennon."

"Wow." The man sat visiting with his wife. I couldn't stop staring. He was engaged in an affectionate conversation with her and didn't appear to be dangerous at all. It was fascinating to be in the same room with someone who killed a famous person. I sat watching him closely but didn't want him to notice. The other inmates didn't appear to be dangerous either. I tried to imagine what they were doing time for.

We didn't talk about Tony's case, because I felt it would have been rude. So I asked him questions about the other prisoners, "Are there gangs? How do the guards act? Are there a lot of gay people?"

I thought to myself, *How does Judy know he's innocent? What kind of proof does she have?* I wasn't sure. Judy was hoping for him to be acquitted in a retrial so they could live happily ever after as husband and wife. Does anyone really ever live that way? I didn't know. But if it was at all possible, I would.

CHAPTER 10

*"Train up a child in the way he should go: and when
he is old, he will not depart from it."*
Proverbs 22:6

The clock on the wall at the Little Valley Jail says six o'clock.
I have finished eating my dinner and feel like I've been awake
for days. The caseworker ushers me out and drives me to my first
foster home. We drive for about fifteen minutes and then turn
onto a back road. I arrive in the driveway of the largest house I
have ever seen. It has a big barn to the left of the house with farm
animals. I see many cows out in the pasture that lines the road. I'm
nervous. The thought of staying with strangers is frightening but
the thought of them knowing why I'm staying there is even worse.
I'm so embarrassed and ashamed. I take a deep breath as we park
and walk down the driveway. A household of ten boys, two girls,
and the foster parents welcome me. The adults talk to the social
worker and remind her that I cannot stay there for more than two
days. I feel so uncomfortable. They don't want me here and I don't
want to be here. But I don't care where I spend the night as long as
I don't have to go home. The two girls make me feel at home and
give me a tour of the house. It is huge and has twelve bedrooms.
I stop to use one of the many bathrooms and I see the largest
amount of toilet paper imaginable. *These people must be rich.* I
feel like I'm betraying my bare-bones upbringing. *They probably
think they're better than my family.* We rarely have money for
toilet paper at our house. Dad's thinking invades my thoughts. It

seems I can't even use the toilet without his interference. He's a voice in my head that never goes away.

The living room is large, with many oversized windows to let in light. All of the kids gather around me. They declare it is time for my initiation. I try to talk them out of it saying, "I will only be here a couple days..." But they insist. Off to the barn we go and when we're close enough to the cow's trough, one of the boys picks me up and dunks me in the dirty water. It's a nice icebreaker. We all laugh and laugh.

The routine at the house is unusual for me. We are up at five the next morning to cook for the boys who are working in the barn. Oatmeal every single morning. I hate oatmeal. I see some good cereal, the kind with sugar on it, hidden on the shelves. "Oh! You have Captain Crunch!" I blurt out. At home we never have any cereal other than the kind allowed by the state-sponsored food program.

"Oh. We aren't allowed to have that," the girls tell me.

"But I can't stand oatmeal. We have to eat oatmeal every single morning? You have got to be kidding me!"

The girls give each other an uncomfortable glance. "Well..." they hesitate, "If you're going to eat it, just don't let my mom or dad find out. We would get into so much trouble."

"Fine, I'll eat it in there," I reply, pointing to the pantry.

After hours of chores, we finish by hanging laundry on the line. It's lunchtime and I get out of cooking duty because I have a visitor. It's my cousin Diana and she has come to check on me. What a surprise.

"Hi, Kelly," she exclaims, hugging me. "How are you doing?" She is so beautiful. Her short blonde hair always looked so trendy and sophisticated on her thin frame. Her voice comforts me. I know she understands.

"I'm okay."

"I have something for you from Travis..." she says with a gleam in her eye. My heart leaped with joy.

"What is it?" *Probably a letter or something.*

She hands me a large golden ring inscribed with a school insignia. This is a guy's ring. "His class ring?! Whoa."

It *is* his class ring. He wants *me* to wear it? What a rite of passage.

"I'd better get going. I'm sorry I can't stay longer. But Travis wanted me to make sure you got it. I picked it up from him this morning." We embrace as she departs.

I long to go with her but my pain is lessened by Travis's ring. Every time I look at it, I feel a tremendous amount of support. It's too big, but that doesn't matter. One of the girls shows me how to wrap yarn around the band of the ring until it fits. She is so impressed. She isn't even allowed to date, even though we're the same age. Everyone here is so nice to me but it isn't home and my sisters aren't here. Nothing can soothe the nagging pain I feel from missing them and my mother. My heart yearns for my mother. I'm waiting for her to save me. We haven't spoken since the day before. I wonder if she is still angry with me.

It's very structured here and they have a lot of rules. One is "no smoking." *I'm going to have a hard time with this*. At least I still have a few cigs in my purse I can just sneak out behind the barn and smoke anyway. I don't need their rules; I will only be here a couple of days.

Another rule is everyone goes to church on Sundays.

"Do I have to go?"

"Yes."

"Can't I just stay here and sleep?"

"No, on Sundays we go to church."

When I was little, Dad could be found at times sitting naked reading his Bible. He was always reading it. I was so proud of him for doing that. Sometimes I sat quietly as he read at the kitchen table, just watching him. We were all so caught up in this newfound religion of his. It was a religion of convenience, bits and pieces of many denominations form-fitted for his pleasure. Although he claimed it to be one religion, he never practiced it fully.

We believed in him. Dad's presence was so strong the whole family accepted his beliefs. We trusted in him to tell us what to think. We were too afraid to think on our own. To do that would be to defy him and defying him meant defying God. Dad once decided some changes in our eating habits were necessary. In order to conform to our new religion, we had to give up certain foods. If we didn't, Dad said we would go to hell and burn. We would burn for specified periods of time, according to our sin.

I was seven when Dad wanted to start his own church. He and Mom decided to rent an office space on Main Street in the small town of Delevan. They were both working for Fischer Price at that time. They had just had their third child, Bree, and things were looking good. The space was next to Aunt Helen's apartment and across the street from the bar. It was a plain space. It had a kitchen, bathroom, and a bigger front room where church was held.

Every Saturday we rolled up our rug out of the living room, loaded it into our borrowed truck, and hauled it to the church. It helped the front room to have a homier feel. Dad made his own sign and hung it outside above the door, inviting people in.

He painted a massive picture of a statue and used it to decorate the side of this new place of worship. He had a dream, and this statue was what he saw. It was painted on a piece of paneling about eight feet high, with some kind of religious meaning. It had dates written on lines that protruded from a body. It was a soldier-like image with armor and the feet appeared to have some sort of metal boots on. It was huge but its symbolic meaning was a blur to my seven-year-old mind.

He was having a lot of spiritual dreams then. I think he preferred them to be thought of as prophecies and visions. I guess it goes back to his old jail days. He told us of a time when a crow landed on his windowsill while he was in his cell. He prayed to make another bird land and it did. He repeated this three times and claims it to be a power he believes he had.

Dad was the preacher, the minister sent to save us doomed people. He even had a pulpit to deliver his loud and rather comical sermons. He flailed his arms and preached to us. We had to listen and try not to laugh. Dad never went to a school for preachers. He didn't have a license to practice anything of the kind. To the layperson, he was just another man out to gather a following and maybe a buck or two along the way, but to my family he was much more than that. Even though the way he preached was quite humorous, a part of me was listening very closely. Sitting in the chairs we brought from home, I could see out the two large front windows. While Dad was preaching, people were walking by. Nobody ever came in.

I believed with such conviction everything Dad taught me. There was a time when Mom and I went to the grocery store and they had free samples of ham that day. Mom was already ahead of me, so I got myself a sample. It was my favorite, too—the kind of ham with small holes in it that are filled with little bits of cheese. I loved rolling up the ham and sucking the cheese out of the holes. Almost immediately the guilt of what I had done set in. I ran into the bathroom to pick it out of my teeth. I thought I would catch on fire right there in the store. I had eaten ham, a forbidden food.

One of the most important parts of our church was the food pantry, which sat off the kitchen. My parents wanted to fill it up with something, anything, just to get started. Carrie and I took the few dollars Mom and Dad had over to the grocery store a block away. We were told to buy one hundred boxes of macaroni-and-cheese. It was on sale.

"How are we supposed to carry all that?"

"Ask the manager to borrow a grocery cart."

We had seen Mom and Dad do that before but always found it embarrassing. This was for a good cause, though and who cared what people thought. I kept telling myself that we were doing a good thing. So at the store we had to ask for help because they didn't have one hundred boxes on the shelves. The people that worked there were very curious as to why we needed so much. We were very grateful to tell them about our Dad's mission and the food pantry that was a part of it.

I was proud to be part of such a noble cause. Every year at Halloween, our elementary school had a parade. Every year we walked down Main Street in our costumes. Class by class we marched down the sidewalk as people watched and waved. That year I was more excited than ever to walk down Main Street.

"This is my dad's church," I said as we walked by the door.

"Really?" the chaperone said inquisitively. He peeked in the window and saw its bareness.

I didn't care what he thought, I felt dignified to be a preacher's daughter.

"Does anyone go to it?"

"No. Not yet. But we just started it. We have a food pantry and everything."

After church, we would take our rug back home to the living room. This went on for a few weeks. Dad's new "job," his latest money-making scheme, was a failure. They gave away the macaroni and cheese to friends.

CHAPTER 11

*"Take heed that ye despise not one of these little
ones; for I say unto you, That in heaven their angels
do always behold the face of my Father which
is in heaven."*
Matthew 18:10

My time at the first foster care home is spent and it is time to
move on. I learn from the social worker that the next family has
only one child living with them, a five-year-old granddaughter.
It's not a long drive to this next home.

The Allen's farmhouse is very beautiful inside. I practically
have the whole upstairs to myself. As they show me to my room,
an overwhelming sadness falls upon me. I realize that I would be
much happier living in a cockroach-infested mess and sleeping in
a closet if Mom could be with me and Dad far away. Could Mom
divorce him and take me away from here? Will she?

The foster parents leave me alone upstairs to empty my duffle
bag. I begin to search my new surroundings. This room is large
and has two twin beds and a radio. Beds. These are something I
don't always have. I notice how sturdy the entry door is and that
it shuts properly, locks, and has no peepholes. The room's many
windows cast a gentle light on the white closet doors. They slide
on a track and open to a closet spanning one entire side of the
room. I wish I had the clothes to fill it. It's bright and cheerful. But
it isn't mine. This isn't my life. The only thing familiar I have is
my stuffed Smurf and my poems. I find myself in deep depression.
I lie on the bed and cry. I cry until I fall asleep.

Hunger awakens me in the morning. I glance at the clock-radio through blurry, sticky eyes. It is noon. I don't think I have ever slept in this late. Unsure if I had broken any rules by sleeping so long, I lie on the bed for a moment and wonder, *Do I wait until they offer me food? Will I be in trouble for sleeping too long?* These questions can only be answered one way. I muster the courage and go downstairs.

I am welcomed into the kitchen, where my fears vanish. The foster parents are hospitable and receptive and not at all angry. They have more food in the fridge than I could ever hope for and they don't have only one refrigerator: they have a freezer in the basement packed full of Twinkies and junk food!

Sitting on the couch reeking of tobacco and watching cable TV is so boring, so I smoke some more and watch more TV. For two straight days, I only get up to eat and use the bathroom. I keep waiting for someone to tell me to get up, do something, "smoke outside, the house stinks." I guess the foster parents don't notice because they smoke too.

After a couple of days, I start to learn the routine of the house and become familiar with the people who live there. Five-year-old Jasmine is a sweet girl. She lives here with her grandparents. She has a bedroom upstairs next to mine. I don't see her much but I really don't care. I love children but I miss my sisters, Carrie, Bree, and Sam. I wish for them a life like the one Jasmine is living. It seems so unfair. Why couldn't all grandparents be like these ones? They seem so caring and loving.

My mind is always wandering. I worry what will happen to my family. I think back on my life and how far I have come at fourteen.

I had a lot of grandpas when I was younger. My maternal grandfather lived with us when I was in elementary school and died when I was twelve. Before his stroke, he used to make dandelion wine in our back room. He had a vat with pedals attached; I would sit there with him and watch his feet make the wine. I loved him.

In first grade I had some friends whose grandpa lived down the street from me in Chaffee. When they would visit him, I would go over to play. We'd play dolls and make up our own version of the musical Annie and act it out in the driveway. One day I went to see the girls, but they weren't there. I always went in the house to use the phone and call Mom when I'd arrive. Mom didn't let me use our phone much. Any chance I could get I would other people's. My seven -year-old fingers loved to ride in the holes with the numbers while I dialed. Their grandfather liked me. I thought he was just an ordinary grandpa. But he liked my urine too. He had me go in a bowl in his toilet so he could save it one day.

"I need it for my pee plant."

"What's a pee plant?"

"That's a pee plant," he said as he pointed to a tree outside the bathroom window.

I had never heard of such a thing. He stood and watched me use the toilet. I knew I had better do what he said. He was old like my grandpa, but being with my grandpa never made me feel this strange.

The next weekend when I went over to look for the girls, they weren't there again. As I walked into the house to call my Mom, the old man pulled me onto the couch. I was afraid, more afraid than I had ever been. He was grabbing me and touching me. I told him I had to go to the bathroom, but his grip tightened. He was holding me on his lap so tight and smelling my hair.

"Let me go. I have to go to the bathroom." I tried to convince him any way I could.

"My mom said I have to go straight home." I said as I tried to wiggle away from him. He didn't let me go. The only thing I could hear was my pleading with him. His harsh silence told me to get away. Right then I peed all over him. He eased his grip in startled disgust.

I ran.

I returned home soaked in urine and told Mom what happened.

"Don't go over there anymore," she said nonchalantly. But the evil wasn't only there. It also lived in the next apartment, only a few feet from our door.

Our neighbors had grandchildren too. We would play out in the yard, dissecting dandelions and licking the milk from inside. That grandpa used to fix old televisions, and by the looks of their front porch, they were stuck with more than their share of broken sets. There must have been twenty televisions out there just sitting on a slab of concrete that was supposed to be a patio. The grandma was in the kitchen one day and the grandpa sat on his recliner. He lifted me to his lap and his hands started to go up my shirt. He looked at his wife to make sure that she wasn't looking as he began to caress the breasts I would someday have. I decided it was time for me to leave. I never told anyone. I never went back inside either of those grandpas' houses.

CHAPTER 12

"The Lord is good unto them that wait for him, to the
soul that seeketh him. It is good that a man should
both hope and quietly wait for the salvation
of the Lord."
Lamentations 3:25-26

It's the second day at the Allen's and a court-appointed guardian comes to visit me. Who is he? There are too many people who already know my circumstances, why do I have to tell someone else?

"We need to discuss what will happen in court," the man states flatly. He settles into a hard wooden chair on my right and pulls out some folders that he places on the table.

Looking at him across the dining room table I ask, "You mean we have to go to court? Do I have to go before a judge? Will my dad be in the room?"

"Yes."

The answer stuns me. I feel like I am betraying my dad by talking about him in front of the foster father and others who are in the room.

"Where is he now?"

The man looks at me confused and says, "He's in jail."

"You mean people go to jail for this?" Silence reigns in the room. I feel their uncomfortable stares. "I didn't want him to go to jail."

"What did you think was going to happen? What he's done is against the law." His statement is so simple—you break the law, you go to jail. It shook my world. I have put him in *jail*. My heart sinks. I don't like having this power. I am only a child. Somebody please take this responsibility away from me. I am laden with guilt to the point I feel like I might fall out of my chair from the weight of it all.

"I only wanted him to stop and leave me alone."

Noticing how disturbed they are at my naiveté, I am even more uncomfortable.

"I only wanted him to go away!" I cry.

I had thought I could just run away, get a job, and live my life far away from him. For a brief moment, I had been the captain, setting the course of my life away from Dad. Now I am thrown overboard without a life raft and strangers are piloting my boat. I didn't know Dad would go to jail. He must be infuriated with me now. This frightens me even more.

Like a student under a teacher, I get a crash course in law and how it pertains to this case. I have a case? I didn't know we had a case. I have a lawyer and Mom and Dad each have one too. This is bigger than I thought. I learn that Dad will be able to get out of jail if somebody posts bail for him until our court date where the judge will decide punishment. I argue with the unfamiliar faces around me.

"Your dad"—the words stung. *Your dad.* I didn't want to claim him.

"Your dad has been paying your friend Lori to flash him when he's at work." Patty lives across from the restaurant Mom and Dad clean at night.

"Your dad has Lori sneak out of her house at night and he waits for her in the bathroom. Once she meets him, he pays her five dollars to press her naked breasts against the outside of the bathroom window."

"Do you know anything about that?" another man asks while the room closing in on me.

"No." I couldn't believe it. But then I could. I remember quietly about when he told me once about making out with another friend of mine. She spent the night once and while I was sleeping, he had his fun with her. He bragged about it the next day after she left. I never confronted her, though. I was too embarrassed.

"Your dad has charges against him for what he's done to Lori too." Apparently he had been having oral sex with her.

"I just want this to be over! I didn't ask for any of this to happen. All I want is for Dad to leave and for me to live with Mom and the girls." I have no compassion for Lori right now. It's all I can do to worry about my own family.

"It's too late for that. Your mother has relocated to a different town and the girls are with her." His next words tore at my heart.

"How could your mother be oblivious to this happening for so long?" In my mind I search for an answer. Through my anger I respond.

"She didn't know *everything* that was happening."

Why are they asking about Mom? The questions sting. I feel a need to protect her.

"What would happen to the girls if Mom were in trouble?"

"They could be removed from her custody and put into foster homes."

"Would we be able to stay together?" I recognize that my words could determine my entire family's future. What would become of the girls? I'm not ready to rip their world apart as mine has been. I don't want this responsibility! I never asked for this burden. *Why does the fate of this family lie on my fourteen-year-old shoulders?*

Mom came home with a new baby when I was seven years old. My love for babies began to take shape. Bree was beautiful and healthy; I wanted to take care of her. I wanted to change her diapers, but Mom wouldn't let me. Later I had a doll and I treated it like it was my baby. My doll was so special. I dressed her and fed her. I took better care of that doll than I did my sisters.

I had two "babies," one for school and one for home. When I was six I had asked Santa for a "Baby Alive Doll." He brought me one and I was jumping up and down with joy. The same year I wished for a teddy bear. Not just any teddy, bear though, it had to be a bigger one. Big enough that I could lay on top of it when I wanted to feel like a grown up. I wanted to hump it in my bed and make it lie beneath me while I did what I wanted to it. I got a teddy bear, but it was only a foot long. Not big enough to pretend it was a real person. I guessed that I had not made my request as specific as I should have. That bear surely did not do. I needed something to feed my rage.

CHAPTER 13

*"If any of you lack wisdom, let him ask
of God, that giveth to all men liberally, and
upbraideth not; and it shall be given him."*
James 1:5

I work on the farm helping the foster dad, Mr. Allen, with hay.
We load the hay and deliver it to another farmer. I have never done
this kind of work before. Right away I find out why he insists I
change from the shorts I am wearing to some pants. I like to work
and have been used to working with my dad. Besides, the foster
father is paying me. I appreciate having money for my cigarettes.
Both parents smoke too and know the importance of always
having cigarettes.

They have many animals, including cows, pigs, chickens, and
bulls. While home alone, I forget to close the gate after feeding
the cows. While in the kitchen preparing a dessert for that night's
dinner, I answer the phone. It's the neighbor and he's telling me
to look outside. Peering out the kitchen window, my hair stands
up on end as I watch every head of cattle the Allens own grazing
in the front yard!

"Holy crap!" Am I in trouble! Another neighbor stops his
vehicle. He is not at all impressed with my ignorance. As he
approaches the door of the house, I am just about to hang up the
phone.

"Where's your cattle prod?" he asks, like I was on the phone
purposely ignorant to what was happening.

"What's a cattle prod? I don't know if we have one of those."

He runs for the barn and finds a long stick. He spends some time retrieving all of the animals and relocating them back in the fence. He then makes *sure* to tell me how irresponsible I am and asks how I didn't notice the herd running around the yard. I feel bad enough as it is. At home growing up we had scarcely any hamburger, let alone an entire herd of beef. This is too much responsibility for a naive girl like me. He informs me he will be calling the foster father at work and filling him in on my foolishness. He stayed true to his word.

It's evening. I'm being talked to very sternly. I don't want to be here. These people expect way too much! I am beginning to dislike them more and more each day, especially the dad.

I knew what to expect from my dad. My twelfth birthday was growing near when my dad told me he owned me. His touching had become more and more frequent.

On Saturday mornings, I used to watch cartoons. On the outside I was a normal child watching cartoons. On the inside I was full of rage and the thoughts running through my mind were almost tangible. I liked to watch "The Littles." I would fantasize that I was the owner of one of those mouse-sized people. I wanted to own the boy one and leave it in a jar it where it couldn't escape. I wanted to torture it by suffocation to show him who was in control. I dreamt of ways to make him suffer with pins and needles. He could be my sex slave too. I would have no compassion for him.

Those fantasies went on for hours. The Saturday morning cartoon lineup also included "The Smurfs." I empathized with their nemesis, Gargamel, and prayed each week that he would capture a smurf and eat it so I could watch.

We had two dogs then. They were pure white, not even a cast of any other shade on their fur. Siberian Huskies—well, for the most part. They didn't have papers. We got the male for free. The female was one of his puppies. Her mom had died and we buried her in the yard. I thought about her every time we played kick-ball and ran over her shallow grave. She was a great dog. She was from an abusive home. She had been kept under a truck all year round. Her white hair was black from the undercarriage of the vehicle. She was beaten also and very hand shy. After awhile, she became more comfortable with us. Mom cleaned her up and soon enough she was angel white like the Lord had made her. She had the temperament to match. We enjoyed her long enough for her to have a litter of pups, then her health declined. Mom and Dad thought one of the neighbors poisoned her to punish them for allowing her to run loose. A visit to the vet wasn't in the budget, so she died. The dogs were Mom's pride and joy. Sometimes Dad would fight with her because he was jealous of the attention she gave the dogs. She was very affectionate with them, hugged and kissed them. She was the opposite with me.

It came as a shock when Dad decided that incest between the dogs wasn't such a bad idea. Barky, the female, was in heat and her father, Keisha, was hot on her tail. Those dogs didn't know the difference. Dad did though. He enjoyed himself watching those dogs mate. When I tried to stop them, I was scolded for doing so. As I exhibited my horror to what was happening, I remember the scowling stare I got from Dad. I had challenged him and he didn't approve of that. That look was all it took to shut me up.

Sixty days later, the puppies were born and they were beautiful. I was so upset the mating was a success. My parents decided to keep one puppy. I had a constant reminder of his indifference. His mission all along was to have sex with me. By the age of twelve I knew it. Did he want me to get pregnant? Did he wonder if a child conceived this way would be normal? Did he even care? Was this an experiment? By then I knew his game. He had been playing it my whole life.

I have learned a lesson from Dad that would take me many years to unlearn. My body is for the enjoyment, pleasure, and use of others.

Upstate New York winters were harsh and long. But nothing could compare to the clean feeling I got when I was outside breathing it in. Sledding was my favorite thing to do. I spent many hours outside playing in the snow by myself. I would rather play alone than with Carrie. Plastic rain boots were all I had to keep my feet warm. They had no lining and immediately turned into plastic ice cubes moments after I'd leave the house. They are all we could afford. Mom never realized they were not real boots. She thought I was supposed to wear my shoes inside of them. But they wouldn't fit.

I liked to tie the dogs to my sled for expeditions to the store. My sled never did turn out like the ones on TV. I had watched the Iditarod and planned to make my own dog team. It looked so exhilarating to be pulled along while the snow slapped you in the face.

Our dogs were so beautifully white and looked so clean compared to the dirty snow that mixed with salt and mud when the plow pushed it off the road. I tied my rope around the dogs necks ready for my journey down Mill Street in Delevan. My plans were almost thwarted when they started to choke on the rope. We couldn't afford collars. I came up with another brilliant idea. I made a harness out of rope and had them pull me with it. That didn't work either. I surrendered and took them back home.

I was on my way to the little strip mall downtown. It consisted of a grocery store, post office, bank, and my favorite, the drug store. They sold incense for a penny each. Cherry flavor was my favorite. I loved pretending I was a grown up. Since I was too young to buy cigarettes, I did the next best thing—I smoked my incense. I broke the wooden stick so all that remained was an inch or so. Matches were easy to find. Dad always had them lying around. I carried my incense like a cigarette. It smoked just like a cigarette. I must have looked ridiculous, walking down the street while it burned a hole in my throat. I was convinced everyone around me thought I was older and more mature because of it. Dad always looked to be enjoying himself when he smoked. Although I saw Dad as somewhat hypocritical, there remained in my belief that he was something special. He had disciplined me to have faith in all that he did and not to question even in the slightest of his actions. So I tried not to. At least not out loud.

On my way home I took a detour to my friend Becky's house. Her mom Nancy was the kind of mom I knew mine could be if dad wasn't around and she didn't have to work so much. I loved being around Nancy. Her entire life revolved around her children. When I was there, I was a part of it. I spent at least a little time there every day. She could often be found sewing something for her children or cooking something for her husband. I watched her when she wasn't looking. I loved her. She was the kind of mother I wanted to be someday.

CHAPTER 14

*"For whatsoever things were written aforetime
were written for our learning, that we through
patience and comfort of the scriptures might
have hope."*
Romans 15:4

The foster parents had been very nice at first. They introduced me to some kids my age. They often let me party with them. I wonder if it is encouraged. They don't seem to mind if I drink or even get drunk. They give me an allowance, make sure I have money for cigarettes, and don't care when I come home at night.

After having my life run by another, this comes as a shock. Once while going to a carnival in town, I asked what time I should be home. They assure me whatever time I got home would be fine with them. This just reinforced the idea that they could care less about me. Why they are foster parents at all? It seems no one cares. I almost beg in my mind for some kind of structure. Am I crazy for wanting it? My mom would never let me do this and I know why! I feel out of control. I don't know the boundaries and so I start to make some very poor decisions.

I spend my first days there smoking more cigarettes than I've ever thought I could and watching TV. At night I go to parties with the local teenagers. A lot of drinking goes on. One of the reasons I go is to make long distance phone calls to Travis. I sneak in the bathroom of the house where we happen to be partying and use the phone. I wonder, *Where are the parents to these kids? Do normal parents let their children party like this?*

Mom and Dad had many parties when we were young. They liked to have poker games and drink alcohol. When people drink, people pee. Carrie and I liked to spy on the men as they urinated. It humored me how stupid they acted when they were drunk. They didn't even notice us crawling in through the bathroom door. We hid in a large closet. As much as they drank, it didn't take too long before someone had to use the bathroom. If our parents or a female came in, we would hide our eyes. We watched the men as they pulled out their penises. They all looked the same to us. They all looked like Dad's. We had no interest in looking at Dad's penis; he showed it to us all the time. He was always walking around the house naked. He ate meals in the nude. It was not unusual for him to be in the buff. He thought his dangling part was something to be proud of. I thought it was ugly.

My parents also liked to have my aunt and uncle over for séances too. This was always scary for us kids. They made us go to our room when the lights turned out so they could try to call up ghosts or at least try to. I heard some crazy noises while they were having their conjurings. They told me about it after it was over, how the phone rang and nobody was on it, or how the table shook for no reason.

Our fears were fed even more by the frightening movies they made us watch. We saw films like *The Exorcist*, *Rosemary's Baby*, and a plethora of other supernatural films that were popular at the time. They instilled a sense of fear and uneasiness about a world I was already so unsure of.

CHAPTER 15

*"That their hearts might be comforted, being knit
together in love, and unto all riches of the full
assurance of understanding, to the Acknowledgment
of the mystery of God, and of the Father, and of
Christ."*
Colossians 2:2

Eventually I begin to enjoy this newfound freedom given me at
the foster home. It makes me feel so mature in a way and though I
still long for structure, I wonder, *Am I too far gone to be receptive
to it?* When I'm alone, I long for a parent. I long for my mother.
As emotionally detached as she is, I ache from wanting her. She is
my mother and there is no replacing her. Why hasn't she called?

After four long days, Mom brings the girls for a visit. I feel bad
for her. It must be so uncomfortable to stand in another woman's
kitchen and watch her be a mother figure to your child, knowing
that she is fully aware of all of your secrets. Mom stands there
and I offer her a dessert. I made it just for her, a butterscotch
concoction that was supposed to be pudding but ended up more
like candy. It didn't quite work out the way I planned, but I enjoyed
the experience of having a kitchen that actually had food in it. I
feel guilty, too, that I have all this to eat and she is waiting for her
food stamps. She had to move into a studio apartment with the
three kids and quit her job since the apartment was too far from
work. The kids will have to change schools again. It's all I can
do to keep my mind focused on forgetting all that they are going

through. I wish they could stay with me. By the sounds of it, their one-room studio is no bigger than my bedroom here.

The thoughts of their situation creep in without invitation and feelings of guilt start to envelop me. I make my mind turn off. My feelings have to go away. If I keep them here, they will destroy me. So I use the curtain in my mind to forget. I'm cheerful to Mom so she doesn't have to worry about me. She has enough to worry about.

She accepts my offer to show her around the place. She puts on a fake smile. I reciprocate. I play with Sam, kissing her little feet. I love the way her baby feet look, so pudgy and cute. I beg Mom to let me keep her for the night. She refuses. I bet she thinks she'll be taken away too. Sam's nine-and-a-half months old and it's a lot of fun to make her laugh. Oh how I miss her laugh. When I'm with her, I feel a need to protect her. I want to fill her life with nothing but kindness and gentleness. She brings out the nurturing feelings in me that I know will someday blossom. I spent some of my allowance on the girls. I bought them each something. Bree now seven years old got some new barrettes for her beautiful hair. She was so easily satisfied. I don't want them to go.

"Mom, maybe you and the girls can live here with me," I say and she looks at me and then looks at the foster mom. By the silence, I guess that wasn't the right thing to say. I seem to be saying and doing all the wrong things anymore.

When they leave, I am alone. My identity, where I fit into the world, and everything that I belong to just walked out the door. I'm left in this unfamiliar, empty place. The anger and the guilt are too overwhelming. I can't avoid the thoughts. I want to hurt myself. It seems safe. Nobody would know that I did it on purpose. I don't give any thought to the whys, only the hows.

The big day is getting close. I don't want to have to testify in front of all those people. I don't want to tell them the things Dad's done to me. I don't even want to think about it. The angrier I get, the more I want to hurt myself. I wonder if I can fix everything by disappearing.

When Mom calls me the week before court, I am allowed to talk to her. The foster mom stands in the kitchen where the phone hangs on the wall. She seems to be eavesdropping on my conversation.

I don't say much though. I only answer yes, no, or okay. In fact, it isn't a conversation at all but a series of commandments from Dad. He has gotten on the phone. I had been told he could not have contact with me. So why is he secretly on the phone rehearsing his plan for our court date scene by scene? He's scared but he knows how to play the system and he knows how to play me. He wants an answer right now, before we hang up. Are we in agreement? Will I lie for him at court next week? I figure Dad got on the phone because he knew he was more intimidating than Mom. He was right. Why does she let him do that? Does she realize what she is asking me to do?

"If you do this one little thing, then everything will be better. I promise. As soon as you see me in court, you have to walk over and give me a hug. Everyone will be watching."

For the first time since this mess started, I have a solution. At least we have a plan to get me home with Mom and the girls. Besides, Dad promises things will be better and I want to believe him. I guess he'll find somewhere else to live.

My caseworker shows up to visit. She talks to me about what will happen in court.

"I have to tell you something," I say as we sit on the couch together.

"Go ahead."

"I lied, I made everything up."

I don't know what she's thinking at this point. Whatever emotion she feels, I suspect it isn't a pleasant one. I have to be strong to be with the girls again.

I thought she was on my side, but now I can see she's not. She almost pounces off the couch to run and tell the foster parents. This is *my* life. I'm only supposed to be living here. Why does she tell them everything?

What gives all of them the right to get angry with me? They have no right. I'm not hurting them in any way. It angers me when they talk about me like I'm some kind of reject that they don't know what to do with.

CHAPTER 16

*And I will pray the Father, and he shall give you
another Comforter, that he may abide with you forever;
Even the spirit of truth; whom the world cannot
receive, because it seeth him not, neither knoweth
him: but ye know him; for he dwelleth with you, and
shall be with you. I will not leave you comfortless: I
will come to you.*
John 14: 16-18

I cut myself on the arms. I do it when I want to stop feeling
like a counterfeit. I may use a piece of broken glass, sometimes
it's no more than the cap off of a pen. I never use a razor because
it cuts too deep. I enjoy stretching out the process; the cut cannot
be appreciated if done in a hurry. I use my left arm as my canvas.
It is easily manipulated into a position of control and then I use
my right hand to do the cutting. I can be very detailed and precise
because I can prevent my arm from jerking away from the pain.
I do it in private. Generally, I am in my room where I can break
things that won't be missed. I use broken knick-knacks or perfume
bottles.

I don't understand why I do this. I know it's abnormal, that
disturbs me, but I do it anyway. No one has ever taught me this. I
haven't seen it on television or read it in a book. For some reason
it helps me to feel like I am real. I feel like I'm going crazy. Maybe
I am. But I know I'm alive because I feel pain.

The foster parents don't want me in their home anymore. I can tell. They are afraid I will make up things about them too. Living under the same roof becomes almost unbearable.

When they're gone, I look around the house for something to hurt myself with. I have to be careful. I have to make it look like an accident. I toy with the idea of using a knife; maybe I will do it in the kitchen while preparing food. I decide not to and head up the stairs. Again in the bedroom that is not my own, I glance out the window that's to the left of the bed that's not mine. I face the river. Nobody can see me from the road in front of the house. I could break my arm by having the window "fall" on it. Besides, I don't like these people knowing my life story and being in my business. Breaking my arm with their window might teach them a lesson. Maybe they will even feel a little guilt for being so nosy.

When I open the window, I realize that my plan is going to take some effort. It doesn't open and close smoothly like a new window does. I don't think it had been open in a long while. I have to get up the nerve, so I take a couple of deep breaths to relax. As I lay my left arm across the sill, I close my eyes. I just want to go to a place where nobody knows my secret, a place of nurturing and compassion. A hospital seems like a welcome retreat. The window does not come down by itself. I have to use my right hand to slam it down. *Come on ... the sooner I get this over with the better.* I'd like to be gone from this place before the foster parents get home from wherever they went. I know that calling 911 will get me to where I need to be.

At first I try slamming it lightly, but that is a waste of time. I increase the intensity. Now this is the ninth crash, I am so determined. I raise the window for the tenth and ultimate crash. With all my strength, I bring it down. I'm stunned. The pain takes my breath away. My arm is broken. The ambulance is coming to pick me up. This is urgent. If my foster parents pull in before the ambulance does, I am sunk.

I wait downstairs, but the pain is starting to go away. In order for this call to be legitimate, more suffering is required. Back up the stairs I go, to the bedroom and over to the window again for one last attempt. Now I stand by the door waiting for the cavalry, holding my arm cradled to my chest.

Yikes! Let's get this ambulance out of the driveway now that I'm finally in here. Here we go! On the way, the E.M.T. informs me he does not think my arm is broken. I have good pulses, my hand is warm, and I can move all of my fingers. He probably expects some expression of relief from me. I try to fake it. This means I am in a heap of trouble when the foster parents get home.

Here they are. Her red hair as wild and angry as her face. His proud stance tells me there is no way out of this one. Now things are going to go from really bad to really worse.

At the dinner table that night, I wear my new sling. They won't even look at me. They don't need to know that I purposely hurt myself. They already know enough.

As I try to fix myself a salad, Mr. Allen looks at me.

"How pathetic. If you can't fix your own plate, then you can't eat. It's not like your arm is broken."

What's the matter with these people? I think to myself.

The foster parents don't take me anywhere with them anymore. Every weekend we used to go visit their daughter and grandchildren in Buffalo. While we were there, we always ordered lunch from a sub shop. They made the best Philly cheese steak I had ever tasted, so I didn't mind going. Now they refuse to take me anywhere and treat me like I'm a leper.

I feel like a volcano that could erupt at any moment and God help whoever is in my path. I will mow them down and bury them without hesitation. The tension is unbearable. They can't even stand to be around me in the house. The father doesn't want me to work with him anymore and the mother doesn't want me cooking with her. The large rooms in the house seem to taunt me with the emptiness that fills them.

It's midnight. I am in my bedroom on the second floor listening to the quiet. I decide it's time to run away from these idiots. Now I'm standing with a firm grip on the windowsill. It's the same window I used to try and break my arm. It's so quiet. I wonder if I will break my legs when I jump out the window. It wouldn't do me any good to break something now. I need my legs to run—run far away from this place. I'll run to my mother who will save me. I've had enough. I can't take the pressure anymore. I feel as if I am solely responsible for ripping everyone's world apart. It doesn't take as much thought this time. I'm not as nervous and the anger I am feeling overshadows the other emotions that try to creep in.

I jump. When my feet hit the ground, my knees hit me hard in each eye. They throb for a moment while I search the yard to make sure nobody has seen me. Thank goodness nothing's broken. It is a very dark night, not a star in the sky. I feel safe in the dark. The area doesn't have any streetlights, which makes it even harder to see.

At the house, everyone's still awake downstairs and I hope the sound of me hitting the ground hasn't aroused any suspicion. I remain crouched in the landing position until the coast is clear. I know they won't be checking my room, they never come upstairs. I estimate I have at least nine or ten hours head start. With my heart racing and a butter knife in my pocket, I run as fast as I can. There is no turning back now (not that I want to).

Once I am a safe distance from the yard, I do like I have a hundred other times, stick out my thumb for a ride. The butter knife I stole from the kitchen is my defense against any madman that might decide to stop. It's been only five minutes and the first car pulls up. What a disaster it would be if they were friends of the foster family. Instead, it's a car full of my favorite kind of people, teenage boys. They're on their way to a party. They inquire as to what I am doing out so late hitchhiking. Don't I know it's dangerous?

"I've got protection," I say touching my butter knife. They seem to disregard my reasoning and invite me to spend the night with them at the party. They tell me that they can take me to Delevan, where Mom now lives, in the morning. I decline and so they take me as close as they can and reluctantly drop me off.

The next car is a gentleman who almost word for word repeats the warnings of the last car. He drives me to within thirty miles of Mom and drops me off.

It's only been another ten minutes until a man in his thirties picks me up. While riding with him I sense something is wrong. I don't trust anyone anymore.

"What are you doing out hitchhiking at your age in the middle of the night?"

"I have to get to my mother."

"Aren't you scared that some crazy person will pick you up?"

"It's okay. I have protection."

"What do you have?" Nervously, I tell him about my knife. He laughs. "You know, all someone would have to do is take their fist and knock you out. You're a small girl, what would you do then?"

"I guess I won't be able to do anything." Now I'm on the verge of panic. He takes a detour from the main road to show me where he lives, just in case I don't get picked up.

"You can spend the night at my house if you need to," he says as he pulls in the driveway.

"Ok, thanks." *I'd rather die than sleep in this crazy loon's house.* In my mind I think he is debating what to do with me.

"Please take me back to the main street. If I don't get a ride within fifteen minutes, I'll come back to your house." I'm not planning on it. But I say whatever I can to get out of his driveway.

One last man picks me up and takes me the rest of the way. I don't know where Mom is living exactly and she doesn't have a phone, so I decide go to the house of my friend, Tammy. Spending the night with her is a relief.

Back in the town where I had lived when I was eleven, I still knew a few people but I didn't know where Mom and my sisters were. I just knew they were someplace here in Delevan. In the morning, Tammy and I try and try to locate my mom. At about one in the afternoon, I find her. She meets me at Tammy's trailer.

Up until this point, I was still clinging to the hopes that she would leave him. I thought she would want to protect me. I expect a hug, and an "I'll take care of you" attitude. I hope we can run away with the girls (bumming churches for money) and live happily without Dad. What I expected wasn't happening, though. I thought she was on my side but I was wrong. I would soon learn what power and control he held over her.

Mom worries about getting into trouble. Her face hangs from the weight of everything that is happening. She looks like she has aged. The black mark that plagued my heart was growing bigger every day. I feel like I might sink into the ground from the heaviness.

"Don't you realize what you've done? You have to go back."

"I'll just stay here at Tammy's house. Nobody will know where I am."

Mom calls the social worker and foster home to tell them where I am. The foster parents have no idea I am missing! They think I am still asleep upstairs. Boy am I in trouble now! Not only with them but with the social worker who is beginning to lose her patience with me.

Things are not going as planned or I wouldn't be in this car headed back to the Allens'. They decide that the best solution is to take away my privileges. The social worker agrees. In my mind I think that she is a joke. How does she know what's best for me? I am prohibited from seeing my family from now on. I am not allowed any visits. I cannot even see my baby sister. No phone calls and no letters to my mother. I would rather have it end. They even take away my allowance so that I can't buy any stamps to mail letters to Travis. They took away my life and the only two people who treat me like a human being, Travis and baby Sam. This life reeks of injustice and I am so fed up with it.

How dare they take away my right to see my baby sister and my own mother for a whole week until court? I feel like I am sentenced to death. The social worker might as well split me open and let my guts spill out, leaving them to rot on the ground. The pain would be more bearable.

Mom calls from a payphone but I am not allowed to talk to her. They tell her I am grounded. Maybe she is calling to check on our plan for the courtroom.

There are ways around everything. I wait until the Allens are gone to their daughter's house and sneak into their bedroom. I steal pennies from their granddaughter's piggy bank. This is no ordinary piggy; it is a huge glass jar full of money. It must have five hundred dollars in change in it—they won't miss a few dollars. I fill my purse, first stopping after I have enough for stamps. Then I think, why stop there? I need cigarettes too. I steal at least ten dollars worth of pennies.

I am later called to the kitchen by the foster parents who had picked up my purse and noticed how laden it was with change. They proceed to have me dump the entire contents on the table. There is no escaping this one, and I tell them the truth, that I had stolen from them.

"You've ruined us, Kelly. You've ruined our desire to ever be foster parents again. We may never recover from this."

I feel so ashamed at having done this to them. It seems I can't do anything right. I am destroying everyone's lives. I just want it to be over.

"Aren't there any other foster homes I could go stay at?" My caseworker informs me that there isn't anywhere for me to go. The county's foster homes are either full or only accepting boys. She informs me that unless I go to a neighboring county, I have no options. In my mind, that is unacceptable. I can't be away from Sam. I am too far away as it is. I have a week until our court date. I decide I will spend a lot of time away from the foster parents. I pass the time reading books out on the front porch. Sometimes the neighbor lets me sneak over and use her phone to call Travis. It is so refreshing to talk to him. He doesn't question me about Dad or Mom. He doesn't ask me the private details of what's going on. We talk about normal teenage things. He's my only friend. Talking to him is the only bright part of a gloomy day that has lasted for months.

I will do anything to be with my sisters. Out of everyone in the family, it's the baby I miss the most. She is the most beautiful baby I have ever seen. Her smile melts my heart.

Secretly I wish she and I could go off and live together. I made a promise to her while she lay on my bed one day. I was lying next to her and talking to her. As I stroked her cheeks and kissed her lips I made her a promise. He will never touch her, I will never let him. I am willing to lie for him if that's what it takes to be with her again. He uses her as a pawn in his manipulative web. He tells me I will be the cause of the breakdown of the family. Now that I have found my voice, it is only hurting people. Nothing good has come from any of this. I am naked, stripped of all my decency and now he wants me to pretend it's all my fault. I will have to take his shame and paint this ugly picture of myself to a hundred total strangers in the courtroom. Maybe it is all my fault. Everyone thinks it is.

Why doesn't Mom take me in her arms, hold me tight and tell me she that she will never let him hurt me? I want her to rub my head and ball me in her lap so her arms surround me and keep all the bad away. But her arms are occupied and her heart is heavy. She has no room for me, no room or concern for anyone but him.

It is again too much to bear. I decide to run away and this time not to Mom. I can take care of myself. I'd rather be dead in a ditch across town than be here. Even a ditch is better than this disintegration of my spirit. Even a ditch is better than being evicted from my own life.

The Allens' grown children are visiting and they know everything that is going on. They know that I have said that I lied about my dad, so they felt empowered and justified to bully me.

I will make a run for the river that goes around the side of the house. I figure I can follow it for awhile and see where it takes me. I can't make my get away just yet though. Everyone is outside and I am being watched like a hawk. They think I might try something stupid. So I do the next best thing, I hide. I was always good at that. I can hide out until dark, and make my getaway then.

The more I think about it, the more I know I have made a mistake by agreeing to lie for Dad. I should have held to the truth. I only want everything to be normal. Maybe if I go away and never come back things will dissolve and everything will be fine.

I woke up this morning thinking I could save my sisters and by dinner I feel I can't even save myself. Unhesitating, I head for the basement. I decide to disguise myself on the side of the dryer under some clothes. Maybe I should hide *in* the dryer again. I remain quiet while I hear my name being called. About fifteen minutes pass and I am discovered by the Allens' adult daughter.

"What are you doing? Don't you hear everyone yelling your name?" she asks as she grabs my arm and yanks me up from the floor.

"I must have passed out," I say, realizing this was a really lame excuse for being crouched down next to the dryer.

"What the hell is wrong with you? I could beat the shit out of you right now for what you're putting my parents through, let alone what you're putting your own parents through. Her words hurt. I almost start to cry but I can't anymore.

"My dad might not be able to touch you, but I can. Who would blame me?" She stands with her fists clenched. By the look on her face and the black eye she's wearing from her boyfriend, I believe her.

"I found her," she yells out the door of the basement that leads outside. I should have crawled in the dryer. Too late now. Oh how I want to tell them that I'm not a liar. I want to tell them that I'm in pain and need help. But I don't.

Once back upstairs in the kitchen, the father grabs me by the arm and squeezes while he pins me up against the refrigerator. I can't believe it. Now he has resorted to violence and nobody is stopping him. In fact, he is only acting out the anger they are feeling collectively.

"What is wrong with you, Kelly? Don't even think about trying to get me in any trouble. We've been looking all over for you." I don't know what to say. *They don't know anything about anything. They never will.* I am so sick of wearing Dad's shame. The pain is unbearable. I want to cut my wrist and bleed right here, right now, in front of all of them and release my pain. I spend the rest of the day in the room I am calling mine.

CHAPTER 17

"He will swallow up death in victory; and the Lord
God will wipe away tears from off all faces; and the
rebuke of his people shall he take away from off all
the earth : for the Lord hath spoken it."
Isaiah 25:8

Tomorrow comes way too quickly. I am picked up by the social worker. "Put your seatbelt on, Kelly," she tells me as I sit in the front seat next to her. As we drive in silence to the courthouse, I toy with the idea of how to hurt myself before we arrive. I have to save myself from the torture of lying for him. My mind races, weighing the pros and the cons. I know I am locked into the decision Dad made for me.

I look at the digital clock on the dashboard and time seems to be passing more quickly than ever. We will be there before I know it. I have to do something quick. I look at the car door and realize it is my only escape. I am breaking inside and ponder the idea of unbuckling my belt and throwing myself onto the highway. Can I unbuckle my belt and open the door fast enough so she can't grab me before I fall out? If only I could make that clock stop ticking. If only I could stop these wheels from turning. She's taking me to a place I don't want to go. I feel like I have only two choices and telling the truth is not one of them. Either I kill myself now and quick or face everyone, including the judge and lawyers, with this deception that Dad has planned for me.

I am so very close to jumping. I have numbed myself to the idea. I take deep breaths and relax so I can build up the nerve. I nonchalantly let my right hand get closer to the door handle. I can feel her eyes watching me. Does she know? No, she couldn't. I place my hands on my lap again. My eyes glance at the speedometer—it reads fifty mph. That could really do some damage.

Ultimately the thought that I might paralyze myself and never be able to have children wins the battle that is raging in my mind. The thought of someday having a family has saved my life on more than one occasion. It's as if the family that I would someday have was cheering for me, giving me hope, pushing me forward. Just the idea of them was sufficient to keep me alive.

By now I know the law enough to realize that the judge will never let me go off to live by myself. The courts have control over me and I am at their mercy. I long to be free like my cousin Tad who died in the spring.

I loved my cousin because he was my cousin and for that fact alone. Tad was a lot older than me. In fact, his oldest daughter was my age. He had three children but was separated from them and their mother. He was abusive to the younger two, once even making one of them walk on broken glass from his beer bottle. His daughter was threatened. If she bled or cried she would be beaten, Tad threatened.

Tad was very unkempt with long straggly hair and dirty clothes. I don't think I ever saw him sober. He was on the drug Valium too. He popped them in his mouth like candy and washed them down with alcohol.

He had been in trouble with the law several times. He even attempted bank robbery more than once. One night he stole my parents' old brown van. My dad was furious. I remember thinking he was going to hurt Tad real bad. My parents must have felt sorry for him, though. They could only stay mad at him for a short while.

One summer Tad decided he was going to live in the doghouse in our backyard, but not on the ground. He put the dog house (that Dad built) up in a tree. I didn't care as long as it wasn't in my favorite tree. I thought it was the funniest thing, watching him struggle with the house and believing he was really going to live in it. He would have had to sleep sitting upright with his feet dangling out the dog door fifteen feet in the air. I don't think he made it more than one night. Mom and Dad wouldn't let him stay in the house, so Tad would disappear for weeks, even months. I never knew what he was doing or who he was with. He never worked so he wasn't easy to get a hold of. He would just show up out of the blue, one time with another man's wife. They were both so drunk and wasted on drugs I didn't know what else to do but laugh at them. Mom and Dad weren't home and I was babysitting. As they sat on the couch speaking their own slang, I watched them. *What a waste*, I thought to myself.

Tad's visits were sporadic. When he needed some of Dad's spiritual advice, he'd show up. Sometimes he would hang around for days, sometimes only hours. Mom always made sure he ate, and Dad always made sure he was preached to. I always made sure I got whatever I could from him, even though he didn't have much.

During a conversation with Dad, my cousin spoke of a dream that had frightened him. He had been alone in the woods when many lights surrounded him. They began to come closer and as they did the sounds of breaking branches filled his ears. The lights were coming closer and closer and the noises were getting louder and louder. Then his dream was over. I suppose he wanted Dad's prophetic interpretation of the nightmare. I don't know what Dad told him but I do know that this began the all-time, most awesome prank we ever pulled.

Tad was camping in the woods behind the school where I drove my three-wheeler. Dad gathered us girls and a couple of our friends. He had us walk to the convenience store down the street to get five books of matches each. Then we met by the school and rode the three-wheeler near where Tad was camping. We didn't want him to hear us surrounding him. He had set up camp next to the pond that was back there.

It was Dad's idea to surround him and light our matches one by one. We cracked branches and lit matches and watched his reaction from the woods. We had almost completely surrounded him and we were getting closer and closer.

"I know that's you, Paul!" he screamed. But I think he was just hoping it was his uncle. I know he was worried his nightmare had become a reality. After a few minutes of torturing him, we came out of hiding. We had a few laughs about it. I think Tad was a little scared.

I hid under Tad's makeshift tent that was lying on the ground. He thought everyone had left, he lifted it up, and I jumped out at him. It was classic. The terror on his face was priceless.

The next day I went to see him in the woods. We talked and I was telling him how I didn't have any money for school clothes and he told me he was thinking about robbing the bank in downtown Franklinville. He had robbed banks before so I figured, *Why not see what I could get out of it.*

We had a plan, or should I say, I had a plan. Tad never planned anything. I found a rock and we marked it by placing some other stones around it. After he robbed the bank, he would leave me some money under the rock. One hundred dollars should be enough and we agreed. Then I started to worry, *What if he got caught? How would I get my money?* What a dismal thought. I tried to stay positive.

Well, Tad never did rob that bank. In fact, later he showed up at the house, dirty as usual, and wanted me to shine his boots. They were by far the nastiest smelling and looking boots I had ever seen. I told him I would for five dollars. He, as usual, didn't have any money, so we agreed that he would pay me the next day.

The next day came and Dad was selling his bunk beds at an auction. I saw Tad. He didn't have my five dollars. I was livid and wouldn't speak to him for the rest of the day.

A couple of days later, I was babysitting my sisters. As I sat on the couch playing with the dogs, the news came on the TV. The screen showed an occupied body bag being carried away from a river's edge. The reporter said my cousin's name. He stated that Tad had been found in a kneeling position on a rock and that he was dead. They proceeded to talk about where he was from and that his last known address was in Delevan, Aunt Helen's house. I couldn't believe my ears. He was dead. It took a minute to sink in. The guilt began to set in about my anger toward him. I couldn't call Mom because we didn't have a phone. Suddenly Gary showed up in the driveway asking if I heard what had happened. He saw it on the news and drove right over. But I had just seen him in a body bag, being loaded in an ambulance. I hoped it was another person with the same name, but I knew in my heart it was him.

We attended Tad's funeral three days later. He was clean, nicely dressed, and shaven. He never looked so good. So good, in fact, my grandma took pictures of him. His oldest child was very upset and we talked outside for awhile. I asked Dad if it would be okay to put a note in Tad's casket. I wrote him an apology letter for being so mad about the five dollars. I opened his hands and slipped it in between his cold fingers.

"He won't be able to read it. His soul is asleep until the end of the world," Mom and Dad said, preaching as usual. But it made me feel better. I believed he knew I was sorry and I believed he was alive in spirit. He was in a better place than I.

CHAPTER 18

*"Then spake Jesus again unto them, saying I am the
light of the world: he that followeth me shall not walk
in darkness, but shall have the light of life."*
John 8:12

The caseworker and I walk into the courthouse. Every eye is
on me now. The pressure is overwhelming. I feel I have no choices
here. I haven't seen Dad since the Fourth of July. Mom and Dad
are counting on me today. I have the responsibility of saving my
family. Dad told me if I do this one thing, everything will be
different. We can be a normal family and he will never touch me
again. I believe him. Dramatizing my love for this monster, I walk
over and throw my arms around him like being apart has been my
curse and I have suffered enough. I don't like to touch him. He
disgusts me. But I can't show any disgust. People watching might
notice. I don't want my breasts to touch his chest in a hug for fear
he will become aroused. I don't want to be any part of this man's
fantasies.

I am humiliated. I know what everybody's thinking, "Hey
there's that girl who said those horrible things about her dad. Look
at her... how can he hug her? Isn't he afraid she might lie about
him again?"

My court-appointed attorney takes me into a room. He is upset
that I have changed my story. He lives in Franklinville, the town
I ran away from. His daughter and I went to school together. But
we didn't exactly travel in the same circles. My lawyer doesn't
believe that I am lying. He needs me to tell the truth. Dad needs

me to lie. I need to be with my sisters, so Dad's plan wins the battle I've been fighting in my mind since he called me that day. It is the hardest thing I have ever had to do, but I believe things will be better. Dad promised it.

Now it's the judge's turn with me. He calls me into his chambers, but he calls my parents in too. He wants to know the truth and this is my last chance to tell him before our hearing. I lie again. I perjured myself and Mom and Dad watched. I can sense their relief. It lies like a light film across my guilt.

There are no chairs in the courtroom. The room is full and bustling with people. Do they all know about my secret? How come the world is invited to watch as I am portrayed as a vicious and vindictive psycho? The bailiff calls attention to the front of the room as the judge enters, the man I lied to only moments ago. The judge begins to talk and starts to make me a ward of the court and sentence me to a home for wayward girls. *I didn't do anything wrong...* I think.

Great, he gets out of jail and I get sent to a girls' home. I can't believe my ears. Dad is standing next to me and nudges my hand with his.

Say something, before it's too late... I think. *What do I say? Am I allowed to speak?*

Gathering my courage, I finally blurt out, "Mmm is there anything else you can do?" The judge looks at me, shocked.

"Yes, there is another option. If your father is willing to not live in the house, you will be able to go home. Your father, mother, and you will be expected to attend family counseling to deal with the fact that you have lied against them."

I shake my head in agreement and Dad does too. *Okay. I'll go to counseling for being a liar and Dad won't be allowed to live with us.* That's what I wanted all along, him to live somewhere else. This is great! I get to go home and he won't be there. Wow, it seems everything is working out after all.

I should have known better.

The next day I go home with Mom to the low-income, one-room studio. Dad was there. I thought he was just visiting. What I didn't know was that besides the two days he spent in jail, he had been with Mom the whole time.

The first two nights I am home, he slept in a car they picked up cheap. After that, he was back in the house full time. There was no escaping him, nowhere for me to hide. He kept his clothes packed in the closet in case a social worker or law enforcement came by to search. *The whole thing was a setup!*

"Somebody might question you girls at school. You must not tell them Dad is living here," Mom says. My sisters and I are threatened that if the authorities find out Dad lives with us, it's us girls who will be split up into different homes, mine being a wayward girls' home. It could happen. I don't doubt it.

I start to realize that things aren't any better here. Mom hasn't been around both Dad and me in a living environment since July when this whole mess started. I can see a change in the way she treats me. She's scared of me and the power I have to change her life. She hates it. She acts like I asked for it. *Me?* I hate it. I never asked for it. I can feel her insecurities in the snide remarks she makes.

"You better not ground Kelly, she might go to the police and lie about you again," she says to Dad anytime I get into trouble.

I can't believe my ears. Does she really believe what she is saying? He had admitted everything to her. Dad didn't defend me. Maybe they think if they tell me I lied enough, I will actually believe it myself. At least Mom's now more lenient on the rules, even though I can tell it's out of fear. I don't like the fact that my parents are scared of me. How did this all turn into my fault?

My entire extended family lives in the area. You couldn't tell, though, we don't act like a family anymore. Everyone is scared of me. Dad and Mom told everyone I was a liar.

I have a cousin my age, my dad's other sister's son, and his nickname is Bug. We hang out a lot and he never judges me. We were good friends growing up. One night I decided it would be great to camp out in the backyard behind the studio apartments.

Behind the complex, there is a nice wooded area with a path that conveniently leads to downtown Delevan. I have a couple friends spend the night, along with my cousin, Bug. Carrie, though uninvited, weaseled her way back outside with us. I wonder if

Mom pays her to spy on me. It is difficult to get away with anything when she's around. Dad is sleeping in the house and is up to his old tricks. He never stops with his favorite pastime, torturing me. I worry he will try something tonight.

I had called Travis earlier in the day. We plan to meet at midnight behind the grocery store downtown. My cousin and friends are in on it. Carrie can't find out. Somehow we have to get her to fall asleep. In planning my get away, I have resorted to propping some pillows under my blanket to look like there is a body lying in my spot on the ground. I use a doll head and leave some hair sticking out of the covers, just in case Dad was to look. I know I have to find a way to keep him away in the night, so I situate everyone around me and I sleep in the middle. I know he won't mess with me when all my friends are around. So I wait until Carrie falls asleep. The minutes seemed to go on forever. My friends and I have a plan .We won't talk to each other or Carrie so she will fall asleep sooner. I have to be at the store by midnight.

Finally she falls asleep and I make my way through the wooded path that leads downtown. The entire time I am expecting Dad to come pouncing out of the shadows from behind a tree. Now that he got away with everything, he dishes out his punishments to me still. I don't need him to catch me.

I remember the first time I ran away. I had a friend and neighbor Tracy. We had a lot in common. She was not very popular with the kids at school either. She was the oldest of three kids and had to baby-sit often. Her mother was a very angry woman who would hit Tracy for breathing wrong if she felt the urge. I felt so sorry for her and wished there was something I could do. Her mother didn't hit her as much when I was around, so I tried to hang at their house. Besides, I liked her and somehow watching her life made my own more bearable. Her mom liked me but she scared me. Her violent outrages seemed to come on without warning. She was always swinging those arms, ready to hit.

Dad and I had an argument. Then Mom joined in. Dad told me to get out of the house.

"You might as well go live with Tracy. You want to be over there so much." I could not believe my ears. Inside I was jumping for joy. This was my chance. I could go live with Tracy and her mother. Perfect. I was standing on the stairway halfway up the stairs when he said it. I practically ran up the stairs when he said it. When he wasn't looking, I snuck over to Tracy's with a bag I had quickly packed.

Wow, what a relief—an instant load had lifted. I thought I was home free. I was talking with Tracy's mom and asking her if I could stay. No sooner did I have my whole future planned when Carrie came knocking on the door.

"Dad wants you to come home." I was horrified

"But, but, he told me to get out." My dreams were crushed. This couldn't be good .I knew there was trouble to be had at our house and I knew I better march right back over there in a big hurry. Of course my suspicions proved true and all hell broke loose because I had actually left.

Even though I had only been gone a few minutes, there would have to be a punishment.

I made it! Just in time too. My heart is racing. It's almost midnight and Travis should be here any minute. I am sitting on the steps by the grocery store. It's closed and everything is dark. A police officer drives down the main street. I crouch down to hide from the streetlights. Travis pulls behind the grocery store like I told him too. He has his mother's sports car. She is out of town and he has the keys. I feel so grown up. We drive the ten miles back to his place. I could finally relax for awhile. I wasn't caught and nobody even knew I was missing.

Once at his place we relax and act like grown ups. We have the whole place to ourselves. We kiss and make out on his mom's bed, but we never have sex—not for the lack of wanting to on my part. I am a virgin, but I would make the sacrifice if he asked me to. I am so in love with him. I never want to leave. I feel safe. But five a.m. comes quickly and I know the sun will rise soon. I have to get back to my campsite while it's still dark outside. They know where he lives now and this is the first place they will look if they notice I'm gone.

"Hey, do you wanna drive?"

"If we get pulled over we'll really be in trouble," I say.

"Then don't get pulled over." He had only a permit and I had only the experience from driving with Dad.

Dad would let me drive when I was young if I sat on his lap. Sitting between his legs was never acceptable. I had to sit on his private area so he could shift my body around when he got aroused.

Luckily Travis and I make it back without incident. I walk back to where we have our blankets laid out. My friends and Carrie are still asleep. The paranoia is overwhelming. I jump at every noise I hear. Once at the edge of the woods, I stand looking and waiting for the coast to be clear. It is quiet, but I have been gone for five hours. A lot can happen in that time. I creep slowly back to the place I was supposed to be sleeping, hoping Dad isn't lying under the blanket disguised as my cousin and waiting to bust me. He's not and as I settle down to sleep, I dream. I dream about the boy who would break my heart.

In New York, school always starts the first week of September. I will be in the ninth grade. *Watch out high school, here I come.* I have always gotten good grades, why should this year be any different? I'm not too concerned about making friends because I went to elementary school with these kids. I'll get to see Travis every day.

I do. I see him in the mornings, but he doesn't see me. Or at least he pretends not to. Why would he risk his reputation with the ladies? Especially the certain few who quietly wait for me to be alone. Whether in the bathroom or in the halls, their hateful glares pierce my soul. Their words pierce my heart. They are full of hate and like to show it to me with their fists. At this point, my anger is hidden to the outside world. I am nothing but nice to everyone around me. It is puzzling why these high school girls treat me like they do. They are bullies of the worst kind.

The school is very large. I am imprisoned in these walls until the 3:00 bell rings and I'm off to another sort of prison, home. I sit in the cafeteria alone, smelling with body odor because I can't afford deodorant. While arriving at school and taking off my jacket, I notice the stench one day. Deciding to wear the jacket all day to cover the smell proves to be an unwise decision. This only increases the sweat I seemed to already be soaked in. I go to the nurse's office and beg her to let me go home. I give her an excuse that I'm sick, but she doesn't buy it. I've used that excuse too many times already. At last I beg her for some kind of deodorant. Why doesn't she help me?

I sit alone in the bathroom stall with the door shut. It's sixth period and half the day is gone. I can't wait until I am old enough to quit school. I smoke cigarettes throughout the entire hour. Who needs Social Studies anyhow, especially with a teacher like this guy?

He's a large guy, with graying hair and he's always dressed in the finest suits. *You can't buy those suits at the Goodwill*, I thought. He looks down at me with disgust. Does he know my secret? No, he can't, but he treats me like the class junkie, the no good girl who is a waste of his precious time. Does he think that because he has money he can treat me badly? I tell him my homework isn't ready. Homework is the last thing on my mind after school. We finally got out of that studio. Now we have an apartment above Aunt Helen. It's survival and nothing else when I get home—survive another day and move from room to room to avoid the Dad as much as possible.

Mr. Gray-suit tells me his class is a place of learning and asks me to get out on more than one occasion. I retreat to my sanctuary, the bathroom. Here I will remain for sixth period the entire rest of my time here.

Sometimes I skip a half day or even a whole day and spend it with my friend. She has a boyfriend who lives in his own trailer in Delevan. We go over there, get drunk, smoke some dope, have sex, and sometimes head back to school. Sex is easy to find. There's always somebody willing to give it away, satisfying my need for love on a daily basis.

I remember not that long ago when I crossed a line I had hoped to save until marriage. It was the next weekend after Dad made me lay with him on the floor. I spent the night with Ena in Franklinville. We went to a party at her boyfriend's house. He was a lot older than us at fourteen. He had a friend for me. It was only us four. We smoked so much dope that night while doing "head rushes," I'd cut off the circulation to my brain by strangulation after taking a hit off a joint. Just before passing out, I'd release the hold on my neck. My body jerked in seizure-like fashion until I caught my breath and my brain recovered. I did that a lot. I didn't know why.

I was drunk and I was stoned and I was determined that Dad would never take away my virginity, so I gave it away to a boy I had just met that night. He took me back to a bedroom and started to undress me. I made him turn off the lights. I was ashamed of my body. Besides, I knew it was going to hurt. People always said it hurt the first time for a girl. I didn't want him to see me if I made any faces from the pain. He didn't know I was a virgin, or maybe he did. He asked me but I said I wasn't. It hurt and I bled on the cot where we laid. When I was, done I stored that experience in the front of the curtain in my head. I learned I could please men by showing them love the only way I knew how. In return, I got a temporary feeling of closeness and kindness.

Dad always told me he would be able to tell if I had sex by the way I walked. So the next morning when he and Mom picked me up from Ena's house, I worried he would know. I just knew he was watching how I walked as I approached the car. I could hardly even go to the bathroom that morning from the pain. *Could I pull this off?*

Well, I did and he never found out.

The girls in this high school are ruthless, especially one girl in particular. Her type never travels alone, though. After a particularly long morning of drinking, Ena and I head back to school. This girl, Liz, has been torturing me every day and I am fed up.

The bell rings for sixth period to start and soon the halls become free of racing teenagers trying to beat the three minutes to their next class. Liz is in the hall. She walks by me scowling. "You're dead," she says. Like I believe her.

I begin to walk away and then I think, *No. Enough is enough.* I turn around and stare her down, daring her to come after me. She does just that and I give her a shove. The rest is history.

I am so drunk I can barely walk, let alone fight. But I still get in a few good punches. I grab her shirt and as she pulls away it stays grasped in my hand. She's left standing in her bra. It's standing room only in the corridor. Classmates are chanting, "Fight! Fight! Fight!" while they enjoy our display of feminism.

Teachers arrive and take us to the office. The smell of alcohol on my breath soon distracts from the real reason I am in the office. Of course Mom and Dad would have to be called. I am sentenced to in-school-suspension for the remainder of the day and three days' suspension from school. I laugh quietly to myself thinking that anyone would consider skipping school for three days to be a punishment. I glance at my t-shirt, relieved that it remains in one piece. It matched my red and grey socks that covered the bottom of my jeans. *I know I'll be grounded once I get home.* Liz is sent to in-school-suspension too. She gets off easy. She isn't drunk. For me it opens a can of worms I'm not ready to open.

The principal asks, "What class do you have sixth period?"

"Social Studies." They give Mr. Gray-suit a call and find out that I haven't been in his class since the beginning of school. The teacher decided that instead of turning me in, he would just fail me. Of course this was fine with me. I don't plan on staying in school anyway. When I am old enough, I'm gonna quit. I have plans for myself, and at this point in my life, school doesn't fit into them.

One part of me dreams of being a mother and a nurse. The other part of me is a dark spot in my mind that takes over every day when I step into Dad's dungeon. It's hard to see the future sometimes. To live or die is a choice I make daily. I survive the moments that need surviving.

Travis's ignoring is painful and I have a hard time letting go of that. I have no explanation from him, no reason. I wish to make him jealous, so when one of the members of the football team offers me a ride home one day, I accept without hesitation.

This could be the perfect way to make it happen. I pray that Carrie doesn't miss me on the bus. I should make it home about the same time as she does. I accept the ride but he doesn't take me home. We stop on an old dirt road I have never been on before. I didn't know his plan to drive me home involved a detour. I think he'd let me go if I ask, but I don't feel like I have a right to ask. *What is he doing?* I just want to get out of this car. I feel humiliated. I feel like it's all my own fault for leading him on. He takes me home when he's satisfied and threatens me not to tell anyone we were "together."

"My girlfriend would get mad at me if she knew I gave you a ride home," he says. I thought he liked me. I guess I was wrong.

I was getting the hints from Travis that things weren't the same between us. His behavior turned cold. Every morning I'd see him and every morning he'd ignore me. After a week I am handed a note by Travis's friend Boner.

"I want to break up with you. From: Travis." It had some more stuff in it but who cared, that's all I can see. That was all I needed to see. My heart is broke and at the worst possible time. It had only been hanging on by a thread. *What is wrong with me?*

CHAPTER 19

*"But thou, when thou prayest, enter into thy closet,
and when thou hast shut the door, pray to thy Father
which is in secret; and thy Father which seeth in
secret shall reward thee openly."*
Matthew 6:6

I have become a bit obsessive and begin calling Travis from
the pay phone at the grocery store. I call as frequently as I can.
He can never call me back, though, and probably wouldn't have
anyway.

My bedroom now is this closet. The walls are an ugly blue.
Everything I own is in here. This is where I listen to my music,
Bon Jovi when I'm happy and Ozzy when I'm about to split. I play
my tapes and drown out any other thoughts as I sing. I love the
echo that bounces back to me. There are no windows, so I am safe
from the peeking. My small space is my only privacy when I'm
home. Secretly, I play with the notion of death.

I can control the curtain in my mind. Sometimes I can unwrap
the rage so fast that the curtain almost disappears. But then I dig
into my head and uncover a need for gentleness.

There is a future for me. I pray every night for a someday I
know will come, eventually. I am going to survive. I know there
is a sacred plan within a part of me. I yearn for a baby of my own
to love and be loved by. This dream keeps me alive—a someday
with my own family, my own faith, and my own rules. A someday
Dad won't be a part of.

How come every time I eat I have to throw up? I tell Mom that it happens and she takes me to the doctor. I never tell anyone that I do it on purpose. After any meal, I retire to the bathroom where I can take my time filling my belly with air. I suck it in and fill myself up and it's easier to empty the contents of my stomach. I can tell when I'm done. My mind tells me when to stop. When I'm through I open the bathroom door. Then an all-too-familiar urge tells me I have to open the door again. I am obsessed with repeating things lately and a little dark spot in my head tells me when I've completed them. The spot either fades quickly or slowly. If I knew how to, I would turn it off. Sometimes when I think the black has faded, it reappears and sends me again into whatever I was just doing. It's like a taskbar on the bottom of a computer screen that creeps slowly across until finished. It controls me. The only way to make it go away is to comply. There is no sense in fighting it. To do so only creates anxiety and I don't need any more of that. I feel crazy and stupid.

When I wash my hands I don't feel like they're clean until that gauge in my mind tells me they are. I feel like I can see and sense things that are invisible. I can see the germs that no one else can because the gauge tells me that my hands aren't clean enough. I know it's stupid to feel this way but I can't help it. It takes me a lot longer to do anything now that I have to repeat things so often. It keeps going until my mind allows me to shut it off.

We have moved again to Olean, New York. I hate it here. The school is large and full of bullies. Every day I hear of another assault that takes place in the girls' bathroom. I decide that going to school isn't in my plan. The neighbor and I skip school and go to the mall. I know that anything I need or want can be gotten by stealing. I only do it when I need new makeup.

We have our court-mandated family counseling sessions. Mom, Dad, and I are always together with the counselor. It was "family counseling." I know why we are really there. We talk about my problems and why I would make up such horrible things about my father. If only the psychologist would talk to me alone, things might be different. The whole thing stinks. It is just another person to please, another person to lie to. I will continue to bear

Dad's shame. So I wear it, like a heavy coat in summer, and it is suffocating.

Ena, my friend from Franklinville, was spending the night one evening. We use to spend a lot of time together before I ran away. Her parents were alcoholics. They weren't mean drunks, but they were just always drunk. Still, they had more than we did. They even had a phone. I was hoping that when she went home the next day I could go with her.

"You can go if you do this one thing for me." I know what's coming, at least in part. Mom has grounded me to the house and said I can't go to Ena's house. She's always grounding me. All I want to do is get away from Dad and she's always making me stay with him. But Dad says he can fix that. To get away from him, I have to be with him.

"Lay with me at midnight, when everyone is asleep. If you do this one thing, I will never touch you again," Dad's eyes wander around, waiting for an answer.

He has been talking about having sex for weeks, and I've been able to avoid being alone with him. He always made it sound like if this one thing happened he would be cured and his fantasies would go away. Maybe he believed that, maybe he didn't. The only thing I could do was pray that they would.

The rest of the day was consumed with what would happen that night. Defying Dad only fuels his anger and determination, ultimately making him punish me far worse. I try everything I can think of to avoid him. Every time he looks at me, I feel naked and ashamed. I feel like a piece of his property because I am. I hate the way he talks about my body and how it turns him on. He owns me. He owns my body. I hate it but I can't fight him. I have nobody on my side.

My mind was in plan mode. I had three male friends from the neighborhood. Two of them were brothers and the other just a friend. I saw them outside about 10:00 p.m. I came up with what I thought was the perfect plan.

"Please spend the night," I begged. I just knew that if I had all these people spending the night, Dad would have to leave me alone.

"I'll tell my Mom and Dad it's an emergency and you guys are locked out of your house. They'll have to let you sleep over."

"My mom will kill me if I don't get home. I better at least call her from a payphone," one of the brothers says. We are standing on my front steps, Ena, the boys, and I.

"No, you can't call. If you do your mom will make you go home."

"Why do you want us to stay so bad?"

"I can't tell you everything, but I'm scared of my dad. If you guys are here, he won't hurt me." By now I am practically on my knees pleading. I know what doing this will mean for them. They will be in so much trouble. Their mom would be so worried. But this is life and death and that's how I convince them.

I thought I was off the hook when Mom and Dad said they could stay. But Dad was a better planner than I.

"If you boys are going to spend the night, you need to go to bed now. You can sleep in Carrie's room upstairs," Dad tells them.

"We can sleep on the couch downstairs. We don't want to kick anyone out of their room," the boys said, trying to convince him. Earlier I had made them promise that they would sleep downstairs on the couch. Now wondering what to do, I turned my attention back to Ena.

"Ena, you have to come downstairs at midnight whatever it takes, you have to convince my Dad to let me come upstairs." I told her that he was going to make me do something. I didn't go into detail, but I think she knew what I meant. I made her swear she would do everything in her power to get me upstairs.

"What do I say if he won't let you come up?"

"Say you're scared and you can't sleep. Say anything you can. Don't leave me down there with him." I told her to keep coming down the stairs. The more the better. I was hoping he would give up for fear of being caught.

"Wake up my mom if you have to," I tell her.

It's eleven o'clock. I can read the fear on her face. She's worried for me. Is she strong enough to save me? I begin to wonder. I could always kill myself by midnight.

"I'm going outside for a cig," I told my friend. The boys were sleeping like everyone else in the house except Dad, Ena, and I.

It's a beautiful summer night and the stars were shining as I lay on the sidewalk by my house. I take a deep breath and sit up, preparing myself for the pain to come.

Bang! I land my head hard against the pavement. I start out soft and increase the blows the more times I do it. My head is hurting. That's good. I like to feel the pain. I stop to analyze whether I can paralyze myself by smashing my skull. Oh, Dad would love that. Then he would only have to deal with my body and not my mind. All I am to him is a body anyway. I can't let that happen. "What if an animal came along and ate me while I was still alive but couldn't move." The thoughts keep creeping in. I take my pounding headache and sneak back into the house.

The clock in my room reads midnight and I can hear Dad going down the stairs. That's my cue. I have to follow him. I quiz Ena one last time.

"You're going to come downstairs in how many minutes?"

"Five minutes," she answers.

"That's right, and what are you going to say?" We rehearsed again quickly before I left my room.

Dad has blankets laid out on the floor. What is he planning on doing?

"Take off your shirt."

"Why do you have to do this?"

"Take it off and this will all be over. I'll never want anything else from you."

I stand there in my bra with my arms closed tight to my chest.

"Now lie down and take off those pants."

"Why?"

"Just do it and take off your underwear too."

"No, I want to leave my underwear on." By now I'm convinced he wants to get me pregnant, like he did with the dogs. I don't remember if he made me take them off or not.

"I want to have sex."

"No." I was a virgin and he wasn't gonna take that away from me.

In the end he settled for having sex with me his own way. As he starts to fondle my breasts I lie in an almost fetal-like position sideways on the floor. My body lies there but my mind goes away.

I check out to a safe place on the stairs. I can see and am aware of everything that is happening, but I can't feel it. It's too painful. It's like it is happening to someone else. So I will lay here and he can use me and when he's done, I will forget about it.

Forget. . . forget. . . forget. . . forget. I repeat this in my mind over and over and over until a more pleasant thought takes the place of the bad stuff and then I roll with it and concentrate extremely hard to keep the happy thought going. At first it takes awhile, but with practice it becomes easier to do. I can forget anything if I try hard enough.

He doesn't penetrate me. I don't allow it. He gave me that much control for now. He is naked next to my body, and he thrusts back and forth, with his penis between my legs, dangerously close to my innocence. He moans and fondles me some more. I lay there like a ball of dough waiting for him to mold me into any position he feels fit. When he's finished, he gets up off the floor to smoke a cigarette. I try to find something to wipe his sticky immorality off from my legs. Dad hands me a towel. My mother never comes down.

"Can I go to bed now?" I say, hurrying to put my jammies back on.

"Don't you want a cigarette? Have a cigarette with me."

The thought of spending any more time around him is nauseating.

I had always heard about the after-sex cigarette. Did he really think I enjoyed what just happened and wanted to share that moment with him? I knew what would happen if I didn't. It would only mean more trouble. I don't need his kind of trouble. So we sit and smoke at the kitchen table in the dark. No words are exchanged and I smoke it as fast as I can.

As I go upstairs, I try to think of what went wrong why Mom didn't come down. I walk over to her room and she's fast asleep with Sam in the little crib next to her. Oh how I want to rip her head off. How could she be sleeping? Maybe her sleeping with me every night wasn't such a bad idea. Too bad she only suggested it to be sarcastic. I walk by the bathroom. I want to use it, but I can't because Dad will feel dirty if I go and wash.

Ena doesn't know what to say to me. What could I say to her? I didn't want to talk about it. She did what I asked and that's all she could do. It wasn't her fault.

"I've got some speed. Do you want to snort it with me?" I ask Ena once I am back in my room. I chop it with a razor blade and snort it up my nose. It burns and some of it runs down the back of my throat. Any pain I can feel takes my mind away from the pain that I can't.

I want to be in the hospital because I know I will be safe from him there. Sometimes I want to kill myself. But I'm scared as I get ready to slam my head to the ground that nobody will find me in time and I will die. The only thing that keeps me alive is the hope that I will have my own family one day.

The next morning Mom told me I was grounded and that I wasn't going to be able to go with Ena. No matter what Dad said or did, she was not backing down. I was shocked and they fought about it. I couldn't believe I went through that hell and now I've got to face him the rest of the day. I feel sorry for Mom for the fighting that's going on. I believe she's trying to do the right thing by sticking to her punishment.

Ena left without me. I sit in my room trying to avoid Dad, when Mary, an old friend of Mom's, knocks on the door. She used to be our neighbor. I trusted her. I needed her help to get out of my house. Before she leaves I ask.

"Mom, could I spend the night at Mary's even though I'm grounded?" I have to get her to say yes before Dad gets back from the store.

"I guess so, if it is all right with her."

"Sure, she agrees."

We were on the road for only ten minutes when I told her everything that had happened the night before. "I can't go back there. Can I come live with you?" I ask.

She didn't know what to say as we pulled in her driveway. Dad must have been nervous when he found out I was gone. We were not even at Mary's house for ten minutes when Mom and Dad pulled into her driveway.

"I can't believe they're here."

"Don't worry, Kelly. I won't allow him in my house," Mary says, comforting me.

Mom knocks on the door.

"Come in, your daughter needs to tell you something."

"What now? What do you want?" Mom says as I lead her to the bathroom so I can talk to her in private.

"Why did you come to get me, Mom? I thought I was allowed to spend the night."

"Your father wants you home. Now what do you need to talk to me about? Hurry up. I left the girls home and I need to get back."

"It's not that easy."

"What. Come on. Just say it."

"Last night Dad stuck his penis between my legs and went back and forth real fast." I can't breathe. Surely she will leave him now. She walks outside to Dad who is waiting by the car. After only five minutes, she comes back in.

"He admitted it. Now let's go home."

"If you take her home, I will call social services," Mary says.

"Mind your own business, Mary," Mom yells. With that comment, she makes me get back into the vehicle and we leave.

The whole way home I am scolded for involving Mary in our problems.

"You know, Kelly, someone's going to be coming to our house from social services now. You are really grounded now."

Two days later, two people showed up at our house to question me .They knew all the details of what I had told Mary. Mom and Dad make me tell them that I made everything up. I do as I am told and they leave just as quickly as they came. We continue on with our weekly therapy sessions for only another week. Then we do what we do best. We run.

One day we just pack up the car, leave school behind, and hit the road. For two months we drive, bummin' churches for money. This time we head south.

CHAPTER 20

"Jesus said unto him, Thou shalt love the Lord thy God with all thy heart, and with all thy soul, and with all thy mind. This is the first and great commandment. and the second is like unto it, thou shalt love thy neighbor as thyself."
Matthew 22:37-39

I am so tired of driving. I just want a home, a place to call my own. Carrie and I beg in every town we stop.

"Can this be the one we stay at?"

I have already missed so much school, I've given up even passing the ninth grade. It's so hard to be the new kid and make new friends. I'm the kind of kid people like to bully. If there is a bully around, he or she will find me. It's harder than ever to make friends. Oh, I wish for a normal life.

We had our adventures, that's true. We've seen Mt. Rushmore, both Disney world and Disneyland, the Utah desert, and the Colorado Mountains. We've swum in both the Atlantic and the Pacific. We've been to over forty states in this beautiful country, but I long to stop running. My entire life has been spent traveling the country either hitchhiking with Mom and Dad or driving if we happen to have a car at the time. We are always running—running from debt, running from the law, or running from children who might tell on Dad.

There is no rhyme or reason to where we stop. It only ends when my parents tire of this nonsense they sometimes call a vacation.

Mansfield, Pennsylvania, was where they decided we'd live this time. Rents were cheap and there was a trailer park with an empty three bedroom waiting for a family like us to occupy it. I don't care where we live at this point, as long as I get out of this car. We have been on the road for two months.

Mom and Dad could always con friends from church or work to help them with getting a vehicle in New York—that's where we always came back to after running. No matter how far away we went, we always ended up back in New York. They'd get some sucker to float them a loan for a used vehicle and promise to make payments. Initially I believe Mom had every intention of paying the person back. I don't think Dad ever did. Not with his "the world owes me a living" attitude. The routine was always the same—get someone to buy the vehicle, maybe make a few payments and then take a road trip and land somewhere, never to be heard from again.

Before we can move into this trailer, we drive from church to church and from one organization to another, like the Goodwill and Salvation Army, to get help with the first month's rent. The welfare department requires an address to start the process of getting food stamps and welfare checks.

After getting enough money for the first month's rent, we move in. Now that we have an address, we go back to the welfare office to get emergency food stamps to hold us over until next month's stamps come.

Once that's settled, the next step was to be enrolled in school. Like every other school that I've attended, this one had its share of bullies. My first day at school, I was already being harassed by one girl in particular. By the end of the day, I knew that she wanted to fight me after school. I had done nothing at all to instigate any kind of fight with her. I tried to avoid her in the halls and ignore her remarks. I don't know what drove her anger, but it was running full speed in my direction.

That day I spend a lot of time in the bathroom thinking about how I could get sent home early. It's strange how going home seems like a welcome retreat from this hell-hole of a school. Mom and Dad aren't home. Mom is out looking for work and Dad is pretending to. I know I will have the trailer to myself if I can get away.

I wash my hands in the sink and wonder how I can hurt myself. I don't have anything sharp. There aren't many options in the girls' restroom but I can use what I have to my advantage.

I don't want to fight this girl and all she has been doing all day is harassing me. She had just tripped me down some stairs in between classes, the same stairs I was contemplating throwing myself down this afternoon. After being humiliated in front of everyone, I headed for the only place I could find a moment's peace, the bathroom.

The thought comes to rub the soap from the dispenser in my eyes. Surely that will get me sent home early. The school nurse can't keep a child in school when she needs medical attention. I fill my hands with soap and hold my lower lids open one at a time and wipe it in. It burned but that made it all the more effective, I thought. I walked down the hall trying to find my way to the office through the film of soap. I know this is gonna work. They will surely send me home once they see the pain I am in.

"Rinse your eyes over here and then get back to class." Great. I just went through all of that for nothing.

My grades suffered and I didn't care. Day after day I played the game. I went to school. I wasted my day. The only thing I learned was that nobody gave a damn. I had to take care of myself. I was all alone.

Then I meet Punk. He's twenty-one and lives a few trailers down from me. I start to baby-sit for his brother who lives in the trailer across from us. Punk would drop by when I was babysitting, I could tell he was interested in me. He has his own car and always has cigarettes. Now I don't have to get smokes from Dad, and I don't have to "pay" Dad for them. This feels somewhat liberating.

After only a few days, Punk and I are dating. We go to drinking parties together and I tell Mom and Dad we're at the movies. Punk supplies me with all the drugs and alcohol I need. Since Dad has become more determined to keep me as his property, I need all the numbing agents I can get my hands on. He doesn't mind sharing me with Punk as long as he gets what he wants from me too. Mom and Dad seem to like him and his family. None of them work either. They get welfare just like us. They borrow anything they can from Punk's dad.

While playing cards with the adults, Mom lets me have one cup of beer—but only one. Punk keeps filling up my glass when she isn't looking, and by the end of the game, I probably drink ten glasses at least. Dad knows what Punk is up to, and he thinks it's funny that Mom isn't noticing. I bet he can't wait until I'm drunk. He'll probably try more of his tricks tonight, but I'm gonna block my door. Since Mom is home, maybe he'll leave me alone.

I am really drunk. Dad throws me in the bathtub to "sober me up." Carrie turns the water on ice cold and it's blasting straight in my face. She is enjoying herself. I have to puke. Mom insists I'm faking and pretending to be sick for attention.

"How can you get that drunk on one glass of beer?" Her words are ringing in my ears after I crawl out of the tub. I can't even respond because I feel like flushing my head down the toilet that holds it.

The torture at school continues. After about a week, I decide I don't need it anymore. I skip every day. Mom and Dad are clueless because they don't have a phone and the school can never contact them. Punk and I go swimming every day and then we sneak back to his trailer and have sex. I guess we are in love. I miss Travis. I never got to say goodbye. So I replace him with whoever is willing. I arrive at home the same time Carrie does as if I have been at school all day. I get the mail in case the school has sent something to my parents about me being absent.

After a month of dating, Punk breaks my heart. I look out the door one Saturday and see him walking by my trailer. He has a ring of hickeys around his neck. I know I didn't put them there. He crosses the driveway and sits in a lawn chair next to his friend, my neighbor. They are both drinking beer. I watch and stare at them for a while as I lay on my outdoor mattress that Carrie and I camp on sometimes. Punk sees me but he's ignoring me.

I have to do something drastic now. I have to get his attention. I pull out my tape player and load up our song, *Honestly* by Stryper. I turn up the volume as loud as it will go and then I sing. I sing our song across the driveway. I know he hears it. Everyone in the park can hear it. He pretends that he doesn't.

So, I play it again and he continues to ignore me. Over and over, again and again, each time trying to make him to come talk to me or something, to give me some kind of explanation, or at least to make him feel guilty—guilty for dedicating this song to me and then getting hickeys from another. I think about his nickname, "Punk." What a Punk indeed.

I feel like something is crawling in my underwear and biting me. It itches so bad I can hardly stand it. I cut my serenade short, run into the bathroom to investigate and make a horrible discovery. I see little brown, wiggly legged bugs. Some are crawling and some are attached really, reeaaally good.

"I have crabs?" I've heard about them but I've never actually seen them.

"How did this happen? How could he do this to me? He told me he loved me. He even dedicated a song to me. Now what do I do?"

First of all I have to get rid of these newfound pets of mine. Nobody is home and I rummage through the kitchen. I find salt, pepper, hot sauce, and vinegar. I mix it all together and scrub it in to my pubic hair vigorously. Maybe this will kill 'em. I have to do something. This itching is unbearable. After slapping this mixture on, I leave it set for awhile, for effect. Then I begin some meticulous picking and shaving. It worked! I got rid of them.

Next I do what any teenager would do. I tell my friend Sally what happened. Unfortunately, she uses the news to gain favor with Punk's younger brother, Billy. Sally was very overweight and Billy wouldn't give her the time of day. She is in love with him and saw this as an opportunity to talk to him. She tells him about his brother and the crabs. Billy tells Punk and a fight breaks out between our families. I don't know why he's so mad. He's the one with the pest-control issues, not me.

"We are leaving in ten minutes, pack a bag," demands Dad. I walk into the living room after packing my stuff to find Punk's big brother (the one I baby-sit for) carrying out our couch and love seat. He takes them across the driveway to his trailer. That set is the nicest furniture we've ever had. It was given to us by some charity store. It was well taken care of and very comfortable. Mom and Dad had just gotten their welfare check and food stamps, so we skipped out on the rent and hit the highway.

"Don't look back, Kelly," I tell myself as we drive away. But I can't resist the urge. Maybe I can catch one small glimpse of Punk as we pull away. I look—quickly, though, before Dad sees me in the rearview mirror. Nobody is around, though, and I don't get to say goodbye. Here goes my life, on the move again, running now from embarrassment.

I hate sitting in the backseat. Dad's uncomfortable stare from the rearview mirror means I never have any privacy. I swear he watches me more than the road.

We were driving down a highway when something on the side of the road caught Dad's eye.

"What's that over there?" Dad asked Mom. It was an African American man lying on the side of the road.

"Kelly, go over there and see if that guy needs help," he demands.

"Why do I have to go? What if he's a crazy man?"

"Quit being so stuck up and go over there and see if he needs a ride. I'm right here if he tries anything." His words are anything but reassuring.

"Do I have to?"

"Hurry up," he yells as I reluctantly get out of the car. I climb over the guardrail that separated our car from the stranger. I wonder if he's dead. He looks dead. He isn't moving.

"Hello, um, sir are you okay?" His head pops up so fast that I almost fall down from the fear.

"How do you, um, how do you get to Texas?"

"How do you get to Texas?" What, are you kidding me? This guy's not right in the head.

"I don't know. You have to go south. I know that much. Do you need a ride?" I was hoping he would say no.

"Yeah."

"Okay, come on. My Mom and Dad said they will give you a ride." We walked back to the car.

"I have to sit here," he said pointing behind the driver seat as he placed a small, long case on the floor.

"Here, Dee, you drive." Dad told Mom so he could keep an eye on the weirdo.

"Are you hungry?" Mom asked as we pulled into a gas station about thirty miles down the road.

"Yeah, I'm starving." Mom gets him a pack of sugar doughnuts and a quart of chocolate milk. Carrie and I laughed. We had never seen anyone eat that fast. His brown face was full of white sugar and I was gagging thinking about how dry his mouth must be. He ate all twelve doughnuts.

"Well, here's where we drop you off," they told the man. They handed him a few food stamps to hold him over on his way to Texas. Later that evening we had the privilege of getting a motel room from some sucker who felt sorry for us. Mom and Dad put the news on. I watched and almost immediately that man's face crossed the screen. The man we picked up earlier in the day had escaped from a mental institution. He must have been picked up shortly after we dropped him off. The authorities made the announcement he was captured and they couldn't figure out where he got the food stamps from or the knife he carried in his long case.

We end up traveling the country again, bummin' churches for money. We wind up back in New York when the summer of 1987 ends. We were in another new town, another new school. I'm in my room—another room without a door. Dad and I have just gotten back from the grocery store. He stands in the opening, facing into my room.

"Why don't you suck my dick?" Dad asks as he rubs his hand between his legs. He pretends he's trying to move it, but I know he's just feeling himself. The shock of what he is now demanding quickens into an unbridgeable gap between us. I have never been asked that before. Where is this coming from? I am stunned, speechless, and full of rage.

"Those two boys at the grocery store were talking about what a slut you are and how easy you are to get in bed."

"I don't even know those boys. I have never seen them before."

"They know who you are. I don't understand how you could suck other people's dicks but you can't suck your own fathers!" he says as his voice begins an argument.

Mom comes home and by now Dad is arguing with me about every other family issue that isn't a secret. He is already now doing to me what he did to Lori. His sickness is always progressing—like a cancer that eats away at my flesh. He is never going to change.

"Why don't you pack your shit and get out." I know Dad and I know I better hide my resolve and my eagerness. He has given me what I have always wanted—to be free from him. I better hurry before he changes his mind. But I better not let him see that I started packing my bag before I heard his last sentence from the living room.

It is almost an hour later. Dad is watching TV. and Mom is cooking dinner.

"Could you give me a ride to Jean's house?" I ask Mom.

Mom and Dad both get into the car and I pull out my garbage bag full of belongings and sit in the backseat. Dad looks stunned to see I have packed. At Jean's house they pull up at the curb. Dad snarls sarcastically, "You'll never make it on your own."

He doesn't know me. I'm only fifteen. I have a life to live and I am going to live it. I have dreams to follow and I'm going to chase them. I own myself now.

EPILOGUE

I realize now that the voices mom was hearing back then were a manifestation of a postpartum psychosis that went undiagnosed or treated. Had it been, maybe things would have been different. I remain thankful for the things she did teach me though. Share what you have with the poor even if your poor yourself and always stick up for the underdog. Even though she couldn't stick up for me, I don't blame her. She mistook her weaknesses for a strength she thought she had. It's proof to me how one life influences another and so on down the line. We are each born free to make our own choices. Dad took ours away. He is ultimately responsible for the lives he changed. Let us always remember to influence those around us for the better and "fight evil with good" as we are taught in the scriptures.

I sit at the sidelines of my daughter's basketball game as she approaches her fourteenth year. I remember a time when Dad use to hitchhike to my out-of-town track meets. He believed in me and that's one thing I carried with me. He cheered me on. Even though sometimes I worried he was only looking at my body parts as I ran, I felt a tremendous amount of support having him there. No matter how crazy my dreams were to others, he encouraged me to reach for them. I had hopes of going to the Olympics one day. He never laughed at me. Even though he only supported my independence during track season, I used that inspiration to get me through. This was a lesson I would and do carry with me to this day.

I watch my daughter and I know she feels the same. She is invincible. With determination and hard work, the world is at her fingertips. I cherish the innocence in which she lives her life. I am aware every day of the possibilities that lie in wait for each and every one of us.

I see my sons and daughters as they hug their dad goodnight. I realize the simple act of loving and being loved in the purest form. There is not a worry in their hands and not a hint of heaviness in their hearts as they love us the way God intended. We love them back the way parents should love all children—with a heart filled with nothing but helping them to reach the potential we know is inside of them. I thank the Lord each and every day for this precious family with which I am so blessed. My children may never know how in raising them, I raised myself. I have lived a normal childhood vicariously through them and they can never understand fully the healing that comes from that. But I can. I have accomplished my ultimate goal to be a mother. In doing so, my children have taught me how—for they saved my life even before they were born.

The scriptures in this book have been taken from the Authorized King James version of the Holy Bible old and new testaments.

The police statement included in this book is written as recorded with the Cattaraugus County Sheriffs Department on July 4th 1986.

Other Resources

To report the suspected abuse or neglect of a child please call
1- 800 - 4 - A - CHILD

National center For Missing And Exploited Children
1-800-843-5678

Rape Abuse and incest National network
1 -800 - 656 - HOPE (4673)

Runaway and Homeless youth may call the National
Runaway Switchboard which offers services for youth and
their parents including transportation assistance as
well as a message service
1-800- RUN- AWAY

Operation Lookout helps families put out
fliers for missing children
call 1-800-782-7335

Prevent Child Abuse America National Office
1-312-663-3520

Team Hope
1-866-305-4673

Justice For Children
1-800 733-0059

National Suicide Hotline
1-800-273-TALK

Some web-sites that may be helpful:

http://www.parentsanonymous.org

http://www.preventchildabuse.org

http://www.darkness2light.org

parent-wise.org

CPSIA information can be obtained at www.ICGtesting.com
Printed in the USA
BVOW071344240612

293513BV00002BA/94/A